HODGEPODGE

A Collection of Essays

by

Brian Libby

Avid Readers Publishing Group
Lakewood, California

Hodgepodge

Avid Readers Publishing Group

http://www.avidreaderspg.com

ISBN-13: 978-1-61286-233-0

Printed in the United States

CONTENTS

INTRODUCTION AND COMMENTARY

"What prompts a sane inoffensive man to write?" asks the Irish humorist Myles na Gopaleen; "....what vast yeasty eructation of egotism drives a man to address simultaneously a mass of people he has never met and who may well resent being pestered by his 'thoughts'?"

A good question, especially today, when one can put one's words in book or e-book form and so easily foist them on the public without interference from bothersome gatekeepers such as literary agents or editors.

In the case of this medley, publication stems from (a) my hope that someone, somewhere, will find at least a few of these items amusing, interesting, thought-provoking, or an anodyne to that depressing world we call reality and (b) the great difficulty I have in throwing out things I have worked hard on.

Let me adumbrate what you are in for:

Essays 1-10 are a contribution to the theory and practice of education. Here the reader—whether professional or layman—will find much food for thought as I bring a lifetime of experience to bear on some of the crucial elements of contemporary high school pedagogy.

An Innovative Grading System solves, in one decisive stroke, all the difficulties of its tricky subject.

The Test of the Future indicates what will soon happen to traditional evaluation methods (unless reason asserts itself, a dubious proposition in any field of human activity).

Lights! Cameras! Teach! is a timely analysis of a recent development found at a few advanced schools.

Project 1812, likewise dealing with cutting-edge educational issues, is an innovative method of first engaging kinesthetic learners in the study of history and then removing them from it. (Readers who do not know what kinesthetic learners are will fill that gap in their knowledge; those who do know should be pleased by the author's progressiveness.)

Testing Kinesthetic Students, a companion to the above, suggests further methods for handling these problematic scholars.

The *Faculty Assessment Form* is freely offered to help teachers whose schools use such things.

An Innovative Boarding School Model is a profound contribution to imagination and creativity in education. Nowhere else have I gone so far in suggesting how to pry the dead hands of custom, tradition, and sanity from the controls of real progress.

On Institutional Advancement studies a key concern of independent schools, which, not receiving the lavish tax support enjoyed by public schools and unable to cover their many expenses with tuition income (however high), must rely on fund-raising.

From A Guide to the Faculty Lounge contains general observations that probably apply to many such rooms throughout the land.

Evelyn Waugh On Educational Reform contains my truest thoughts on the subject.

Essays 11-13 are a commentary on the nutritional advice we are all ceaselessly bombarded with. *Bon appétit*!

Essay 14, *Just What the Doctor Ordered*, should be of interest to those who take prescription medications (i.e. almost everyone these days).

Essays 15-18 are commentaries on famous films and books:

Historical Films commends or censures various works for their value as portrayals of real events.

Star Wars I-III and *The Choices of Master Peter* are criticisms of films that, despite their popularity, prove to me that the ability to direct a film is not always accompanied by the ability to write a screenplay, and that advances in CGI techniques threaten to mesmerize film makers into mistaking show for substance.

Harry Potter and the Writing of Fiction is a brief evaluation of the strengths and weaknesses of this popular series of novels.

Essay 19, *The Dome*, commemorates the erection of a huge inflated field house at Shattuck-St. Mary's School in Minnesota. This wondrous air-bag, the second largest such structure in the state, seemed worthy of an ode, but, since the school neglected to have a poet laureate write one, I decided to supply the need unasked.

Essays 20-22: these bits of *jeu d'esprit* need no explanation.

Essay 23, *The Adventure of the Surprising Ending*, my only piece of 'fan fiction,' is an affectionate parody of that most excellent TV series, *Agatha Christie's Poirot* (starring David Suchet, whose portrayal of the greatest detective in the world is so definitive that no one need ever play that role again). Those who have not seen it will, I hope, lose no time in watching at least some of the seventy episodes.

Essay 24, *A Cautionary Tale*, meant for the edification of fledgling novelists, is a piece of non-fiction. Unfortunately.

Essay 25, *A Peninsular Battle*, a light-hearted spoof, was written many years ago for the delectation of military historians, who can amuse themselves finding its deformed allusions and misused terms. No insult is intended towards any real units, especially any British regiments that might happen to have the numbers I randomly chose. (That last sentence may very soon be meaningless: the determined efforts of successive British governments should presently destroy the glorious heritage of the British army by consolidating its few hundred remaining combat troops into a single battalion containing such units as the "Platoon of Guards" and the "Highland Squad." But the government will probably keep military bands at full strength.)

*

On with the show!

PS - This book is copyrighted, but anyone may freely distribute individual essays by any means so long as I am credited with authorship and the distributor makes no money.

1. AN INNOVATIVE GRADING SYSTEM

The traditional grading system uses the letters

> A
> B
> C
> D
> F

When students receive a low grade—and, these days, "low grade" often means, in the minds of parents and students, anything below an A- —it causes misery, humiliation, and discontent.

How can we can solve this problem? One way would be for schools to insist that students work hard, to put academics first, to emphasize that learning and studying are not invariably fun or diverting, and that it is in the nature of things that not everyone can do well in academics, any more than everyone can do well in, say, music, sports, or painting. But so severe an attitude is today obsolete, particularly at financially precarious independent schools that wish to retain all their students at almost any price.

Here is a grading scale that entirely solves the problem:

> A+
> A^3
> A^2
> A
> A-

Another problem is that the numerical equivalents for the letter grades are 4, 3, 2, 1, 0. This also depresses weak students (and their parents), who of course want a high GPA. This difficulty too is easily solved:

$$A+ = 4.0$$
$$A^3 = 3.9$$
$$A^2 = 3.8$$
$$A = 3.7$$
$$A- = 3.6$$

Thus no student will ever have a GPA lower than 3.6 and everyone will be happy.

☺   ☜ (Everyone being happy)

Observe how imagination and creativity solve problems that have puzzled generations of pedagogues! We must learn to think outside the box. In fact, we should throw the box away.

2. THE TEST OF THE FUTURE

EUROPE 1870-1945   20 Points   Name:
(Senior Elective)

ESSAY. (4 points) (Do on separate sheet)

Write at least three sentences (or fragments) showing that Adolf Hitler was not a nice man.

(If you prefer, you may write about Joseph Stalin).

CHRONOLOGY. Arrange these important battles of World War I in the order they occurred by numbering them from 1 to 5 (1 being the earliest event, 2 the second, 3 the third, and so on all the way to 5, which is the last.) (5 pts.)

_____ The 9th Battle of the Isonzo

_____ The 3rd Battle of the Isonzo

_____ The 7th Battle of the Isonzo

_____ The 11th Battle of the Isonzo

_____ The 5th Battle of the Isonzo

TRUE/FALSE. (1 point each.)

_____ Russia is bigger than Belgium.

_____ Benito Mussolini was Italian.

_____ Germany and Japan lost World War II.

_____ Many people died in World War I

_____ Belgium is not bigger than Russia

3

IDENTIFICATIONS. Do any <u>one</u>. Skip any <u>four</u>. (4 points.) Do on separate sheet.

1. The Battle of Caporetto

2. The Blomberg-Fritsch Crisis

3. The Beer Hall Putsch

4. The Reichstag Fire

5. Your mother

GEOGRAPHY. (2 pts.) Put these items on the accompanying map, using the numbers.

1. Land   2. Water

Kinesthetic students may, instead of taking the test, perform an interpretative dance on the Battle of Verdun or the Stock Market Crash.

4

3. LIGHTS! CAMERAS! TEACH!

by Cecil B. DeLibby

Revolutionary improvements in education now happen every few months. This year saw yet another giant step: the installation in classrooms of video cameras coupled with Panopto, a program that allows us to store the films of our classes for instant viewing on computers. Being a man who ardently embraces all advances in our ancient profession, I naturally wish to be among the harbingers of progress by examining the implications of this latest breakthrough. What can we expect to happen?

First will come changes in titles and terminology, something we are very used to anyway. The Director of Studies, now termed the "Casting Director," will place job listings in *Variety* as well as traditional locations and will assemble the "cast" (faculty) for the year's "shoots" (classes). An "actor" (teacher), before going "on stage" (to the classroom), will report "in costume" (dress code) before "call-time" (the bell) to the "green room" (faculty lounge), where a make-up artist will insure that the actor does not look pasty or off-color while the cameras are rolling.

During the opening faculty meetings, actors will receive instruction on the key skills of modern pedagogy, such as how to present one's best profile, voice projection, and the importance of not looking at the camera.

Because the presence on-set of real students is not always necessary—they can watch the movie later—the stage can sometimes be filled by "extras" chosen to personify whatever goals the school is trying to emphasize (e.g. gender balance, multicultural diversity). Extras will be controlled by an off-screen AD (assistant director), who will coach them in simulating interest, taking notes, holding vigorous (but polite) discussions, and otherwise impersonating ideal students in an ideal classroom. This will make for boffo kudos when the movies are displayed, as they surely will be, on You Tube as well as Moodle.

As the actors build up fan bases and viewers, Producers and Directors (Boards of Trustees and Headmasters) must expect certain difficulties. The most successful actors will get agents, of course, so the annual contract-signing, at present a simple response to an e-mail, will involve heated negotiations for salary, housing, and perhaps perks like chauffeured limousines, luxurious trailers, stars painted on classroom doors, and chairs with names on their backs. Directors will start hearing things like "I'm not thrilled by the script for Physics—can you do a re-write?" "I'm not right for Middle School Spanish—I'm better with more mature audiences," "Come on, even Sir Alec Guinness couldn't mine any yocks from Calculus AB!" "If I go into much detail about the September Massacres of 1792, will we lose our G Rating?" or "This is live theater, remember. How much audience response can you expect anyone to get from this '*Passé Composé*' shtick?" And don't forget residuals every time a film is played, and fees for "The Best Of" compilations.

Thespians who specialize in the liberal arts will have an inherent advantage over those in math and science: English Dept. actors work with material written by geniuses, while those on the nonfiction side can entertain their students with the antics of various zanies, lunatics, and fascinating homicidal maniacs who so dominate the genre called History. Actors who must try to make audiences warm to verb forms, invisible particles, or complex formulas may demand higher pay on that account.

No school will wish to hire anyone who is unsightly or who lacks stage presence. It will do a school no good to place some gargoyle on stage, however skilled a teacher he might be. Maybe some careers can be salvaged by plastic surgery. But there will be many opportunities for character actors. A media-savvy school will try to present, through its films, a variety of interesting types to provide a potpourri of diverting performances. Among these are:

The Young Progressive: Chummy with students, affects coolness (odd ties and belts, perhaps a tattoo or flamboyant beard), makes up for inexperience by enthusiasm (shouting, prancing about, standing on chairs), avoids giving many tests or "high stakes" evaluations.

The Matriarch: A motherly beldam who brings cookies and bags of sweets to class, perches stuffed animals on the windowsills, and punishes severely the tiniest disturbance.

The Jock: Personable, magnetic; easily distracted from his subject (usually "social studies," which, of course, anyone can teach) by questions about the most recent "big game;" happy to speculate in class on the prospects of this or that professional team in some upcoming tournament. Knows all the major sports stars even if he is hazy on Robespierre.

Mr. Chips: To meet the expectations of the public, prep schools especially must have a couple of antiques pottering about the place, confusing names and faces and reminiscing of antediluvian times. These absent-minded codgers are often a bit weak on classroom discipline and reporting attendance and quite easy to fool; on the other hand, students who enter their classrooms intent on actually learning something often emerge very well prepared for college.

*

A seminal article like this cannot be expected to deal with every change that filming classes will bring about, such as post-production (insertion of special effects and a musical score; editing out such things as an actor throwing an eraser at an annoying student), but the author hopes he has at least given his colleagues food for thought. (Might we eventually progress to "blue screen" classes, where no students are needed since they will be computer-generated afterwards?) We invite you to meditate on this and develop your own notions.

Perhaps it is a good idea to end a treatise about this latest revolution in education with a reminder that the basic needs of good teaching were developed not in 2011 (flipped classes) nor in 2007 (Panopto) nor in 2006 (blended learning) nor in 1991 (smartboards) nor in the 1980s (computers) nor in the 1960s (television) nor in the 1940s (filmstrips) nor even in 1454 (the printing press), but around 430 BC, when Socrates demonstrated that the essentials are (1) a knowledgeable and enthusiastic instructor, (2) students who want to learn, and (3) adequate time. (He didn't even use chalk!)

4. PROJECT 1812:
HISTORY FOR THE KINESTHETIC LEARNER

A Modest Proposal

INTRODUCTION
Teaching history to kinesthetic high-schoolers is challenging because history is usually studied by reading and listening; to learn history has heretofore meant using books, or hearing about events from savants who, having devoted their lives to such study, can highlight, and simplify complex matters for easy reception by tender minds.[1] Now, however, with students who find it difficult to learn by such antique methods, modern pedagogues must develop new rubrics, new praxis, new epistemologies.[2]

We present here an exemplary project that we hope will stimulate many other educational professionals ("teachers") to develop and expand innovative methodologies.

PROJECT 1812

OVERTURE
One of the most dramatic and important events of the early 19th Century was the French invasion of Russia. Project 1812 focuses on the catastrophic dénouement of this, the largest military operation before World War I, which set in motion the downfall of the First Empire and the victory of the reactionary regimes of the Age of Metternich (1815-1848).

The retreat from Moscow has often been described—e.g. Tolstoy's magnificent treatment in *War and Peace*—but how can one bring the reality of what happened to people who cannot readily comprehend the written or the spoken word? We think we have found a way.

METHODOLOGY
Most Modern European/Western Civ. courses reach the second half of the Napoleonic Era in December or early January, which is the perfect—indeed, the only—time when this Project can be properly conducted.

➔ On a very cold day with high wind chill, all the kinesthetic learners will be driven to a mall or other public location about five miles from campus. They may wear only light summer clothing, such as T-shirts, shorts, cotton slacks, and sandals. Each will receive a sandwich, a pint of bottled water, and a knapsack containing about fifty pounds of hockey pucks.

Rationale: The flimsy clothing and scanty food simulate the dress and rations of most French soldiers during the retreat from Moscow. The knapsacks simulate the vast assortment of loot that the French took from the ruined city, confident that they could bring it back to France.

➔ The students will be told they will get $1 for each hockey puck they bring to campus.

Rationale: Students will experience the common dilemma of greed vs. reason, in that they must decide whether, and when, to lighten or discard the valuable but heavy knapsacks in order to have a better chance of reaching home.

➔ The students will walk back to campus.

➔ It is highly desirable that a number of local people be invited to take part in the Project. Their job is to follow the students, and, when any fall behind the main body by more than fifty yards, to beat them with clubs, pelt them with stones, or throw them into ponds.

Rationale: The citizens simulate the Russian peasants and Cossacks who followed the French army from a safe distance but attacked stragglers.

➔ A teacher will ride beside the students in a chauffeur-driven car, calling out encouragement to his "troops" and composing bombastic "official bulletins" announcing that the campaign is going very well. (To assist with the bulletins, he may be accompanied by a "chief of staff" provided by the Office of Institutional Advancement.) When his limousine is half a mile from the school, he will wave encouragingly to the freezing remains of his "army" and be driven quickly back to campus, leaving his men to finish the trek on their own.

Rationale: The teacher simulates Napoleon, who departed the army in a swift coach on December 5, two weeks before the epic retreat ended.

➔Those students who reach campus will be given a cup of hot chocolate and sent to the hospital. The others will be buried.

OUTCOMES

The 1812 Project gives haptic learners a "hands-on" experience like no other. Instead of merely looking at artifacts in a museum or using colored markers to occupy their fidgety fingers, they will feel they have actually participated in an important historical event. It is an experience they will remember to the ends of their lives. (This is especially true for those who do not reach campus, since their lives and the Project will end simultaneously.) At least half of the survivors will have permanent "memory triggers" right on their bodies (such as the stumps of frostbitten fingers and toes after amputation at the hospital).[3] No need for hard-to-read books or boring lectures to teach *them* what happened!

ENRICHMENT

Hardy kinesthetics who insist on remaining at the school after Project 1812 will take part in Project 1941, "Hitler's Retreat From Moscow," which is very similar to Project 1812 except that the local people may use rifles.

Schools in warm climates may obtain satisfactory results from Project 1917 (The Project to End Projects), a simulation of Passchendaele (3rd Ypres). It takes place in soft, muddy ground in early spring or late autumn. (Project 1917 provides a fine opportunity for some cross-disciplinary activity: for added realism, the Science Department can manufacture phosgene and mustard gas for use as the kinesthetics slog through the knee-deep mud towards distant, unattainable objectives.)

----

1 Kinesthetic (or "haptic") learners are those who, we are told, cannot learn much from reading or listening, but who learn best by doing things with their hands and the movement of their bodies. Some laymen, ignorant of current pedagogical "best practice," might think that such students would not be enrolled in preparatory schools or aspire to college diplomas, but would instead be directed into shop classes, vo-techs, the lower enlisted ranks of the armed forces, and similar places where they could use their talents to best advantage without cluttering up the halls of academe; but that is not the case today.

2 I do not really know what these last words mean, but I have noticed that the most esteemed educational experts and holders of Doctorates of

Education use them quite a bit. I thought I should use them too, so I will be taken seriously.

3   For these, the "hands-on" experience can also be a "hands-off" experience!

5. TESTING KINESTHETIC STUDENTS

In my previous monograph, *Project 1812*, I suggested a method for insuring that kinesthetic high school students learn unforgettable lessons in history without the necessity of doing things for which they are not best suited, such as reading and writing. Here I propose a method for administering tests to kinesthetics.

The whole idea of testing is, of course, undergoing scrutiny and debate. It does not seem too far-fetched to suggest that in many schools—certainly in those progressive institutions that so rightly put a premium on innovation and creativity—the notion that students should periodically have to undergo exhausting, psychologically painful, and possibly humiliating ordeals in which they are expected to know things, and to demonstrate this knowledge by writing some of it down, will soon be as passé as slide projectors, mimeograph machines, and lectures, replaced by a portfolio system or a group project system or anything that will remove the necessity for schools to differentiate industriousness, ability, or intelligence, or award low grades to anyone.

However, until that happy day arrives, "traditional" testing will be a major component of high school classes. But how can such tests be made fairer for kinesthetic students, whose learning style makes laboriously studying famous people, notable events, crucial dates, and cause-and-effect relationships very difficult? An innovative pedagogy surely will not try to make these students overcome their weaknesses, but will take advantage of their strengths.

I propose the adoption of ☞**Scavenger Tests**☜ for the use of kinesthetics.

Students certified by the school psychologist, psychiatrist, "counselor," astrologer—whatever functionary identifies some young persons as more comfortable using their hands than their heads—will be tested in a separate place. The teacher will distribute the test, which will be the same as that being administered somewhere else to the visual and verbal learners. However, the kinesthetics need not write anything on the test. Instead, the answers to the various questions will have been printed on little pieces of paper and hidden throughout the room: in books, behind classroom furniture, under the rug, inside light fixtures, etc. etc. The students will leap from their archaic, confining desks and scurry about to find these answers. When a student finds an answer, he will go to his desk and staple it next to the corresponding question. Think how much fun this will be for the kinesthetics: they can use the motion of their bodies and their tactile curiosity to complete the test without having more than a rudimentary knowledge of the subject being tested!

Tests of course vary in difficulty, from basic quizzes to final exams (in those reactionary schools that have not yet abolished such ghastly ordeals as final exams). The mechanics of a Scavenger Test do not vary, but the challenge can be enhanced by increasing the area in which the answers are hidden. Instead of only the classroom, answers can be secreted in corridors; on other floors; in bushes, flower beds, and other campus flora; in administrative offices; perhaps in a drawer in the Headmaster's desk. The haptic learners will then have a really kinetic evaluational experience as they ransack the entire school to find them. (This can be a learning experience for the whole school community, too, which can live through a simulation of the sack of Jerusalem in 1099 or the Spanish Fury at Antwerp in 1576.)

Thus a Scavenger Test can be varied in difficulty from a mild "Easter Egg Hunt" to a cataclysm that leaves the school looking like northern France in 1918.

*

The "basic" Scavenger Test presupposes that the number of answers is sufficient for all the students to get an A+ : i.e. if there are nine students being tested, nine copies of each answer will be hidden. But those schools interested in introducing an element of real-world competitiveness into testing—for seniors, perhaps, about to leave the loving, caring coddling of an innovative and creative private school for the reality outside— can easily simulate this by simply making fewer answers available than there are students. Imagine the enhanced excitement generated by telling several seniors, their competitiveness and aggression already honed to a razor's edge by years of playing sports, that there is only one hidden answer to each ID question. The result should be exceedingly kinetic. And the mayhem may reduce the number of kinesthetics at the school— which, readers may recall, was also one purpose of *Project 1812*.

6. FACULTY ASSESSMENT FORM

Student Course Evaluation for: _____

Please circle the number that best reflects your opinion.

Key: 1= Disagree 2 = Mildly disagree 3 = Agree   **4 = Agree Strongly**

1. This course is wonderful.	1 2 3	4
2. The teacher is wonderful.	1 2 3	4
3. The school is wonderful.	1 2 3	4
4. Tests are returned before they are taken.	1 2 3	4
5. Homework is interesting, challenging, and takes less than ten minutes to do.	1 2 3	4
6. Extra help is available 24/7. The teacher has no personal life at all.	1 2 3	4
7. The course doesn't interfere with sports very much.	1 2 3	4
8. Extra-credit is readily available for F students.	1 2 3	4
9. The teacher combines the best qualities of Socrates, Gandhi, and Einstein.	1 2 3	4
10. The teacher deserves a large raise.	1 2 3	4
11. The teacher deserves a nicer house.	1 2 3	4
12. The teacher should be given a school car.	1 2 3	4
13. The teacher deserves a year-long sabbatical.	1 2 3	4

Optional Comments. (Use other side)

(All comments must include the words "brilliant," "compassionate," "superb," "genius," and/or "relevant.")

14

7. AN INNOVATIVE BOARDING SCHOOL MODEL

In the very competitive world of college-preparatory boarding schools it is essential that a school have a character, a distinctive personality, traits that distinguish it from similar institutions. At least two decades ago a highly-respected consultant told us that a "plain-vanilla" school—one that offered merely a traditional program of strong academics—would have a hard time selling itself to prospective customers.[1]

It is also clear that, given the tremendous amount of thought and work that many fine schools have put into designing distinctive programs, it is becoming harder and harder to "think outside the box" because the box is now so large. Cutting-edge technology courses are common; unusual language programs—Chinese, Tagalog, Finnish, whatever—are jejune. (Even some *public* schools teach Mandarin, so plebeian has it become!) Transforming a school into a sports academy is hardly noteworthy (though still very tragic).

No, what is needed is something really progressive, truly innovative, authentically revolutionary. And here it is: the non-residential boarding school (NORBS).

The advantages of such a school to the board of trustees or proprietor are obvious. There is no need for dormitories, athletic facilities, laboratories, a chapel, a large cafeteria, or more than a few classrooms. Outlay is limited to the upkeep of a couple of buildings and some teachers (the latter being, of course, an almost trivial expense). All the rest of the money can go to paying vast sums to administrators, as it should.

But how would such a school exist? Surely this is some silly fantasy? No, no, not at all. Now that the computer and its associated applications exist, now that we have the means of instant communication, the non-residential boarding school is quite possible. Let us describe its main features:

15

ACADEMICS

We do not propose the usual form of "distance learning" in which students listen to lectures or watch demonstrations randomly and at their own convenience. No. Each student will have a class schedule. At, let's say, 9 AM, everyone in a given section of English III [or Language Arts III, for those schools that have gone over to the Dark Side] will stand before their computers with webcams trained on themselves. The teacher—or perhaps a dean—will inspect the class to insure that each student is in dress code, instructing those who are wrongly attired to go change and awarding demerits to repeat offenders.

The teacher will then teach the class. Students with questions will push a button to notify the teacher, who can respond as is convenient.

The teacher will be in a normal classroom facing some sort of camera.[2] It should be possible for the students to be displayed on a wall-sized array of screens. If this is not possible, a "virtual class" can be projected on the wall so the teacher has the illusion of speaking to real people. (Holographic projection of 3-D students at desks will be used when technology permits.)

If the class involves discussion, students can 'text' messages that will be displayed to everyone. Skype should also be useful. Science classes will of course use online virtual labs to carry out experiments, dissections, etc.

At the end of class a virtual bell will ring out. Students then have five minutes to log in to their next class. Students with study halls will sit in front of their webcams with Kindles, iPads, Blackberries, Mulberries, or even with books, monitored by the study hall teacher.

EVALUATION

Possibly some readers are wondering how tests will be given in a NORBS. Let me happily inform the ignorant layman that the world of education is rapidly moving away from the "test." The notion that evaluation basically means that a student studies something, learns it as best he can, and then demonstrates that knowledge on a timed written or oral exercise that is graded as to its quality, is becoming obsolete. Such "high-stakes tests"—and apparently all tests are such; I have yet to hear the term "low-stakes test"—are potentially damaging to self-esteem, unfair (being biased in favor of smart, industrious people), and generally icky. Indeed the whole notion that students should 'know' anything is almost passé among the pedagogical pioneers who are improving education every week. After all, one can surely look up any mere facts on Wikipedia.

Consequently we assume that—until the happy day when newborns receive bachelor's degrees along with their birth certificates in a perfectly egalitarian society—the necessary 'grading' will be done on the basis of class participation, group participation, mastery of learning skills, class effort, sense-making, portfolios, concept checks, and self-evaluations using detailed rubrics for each category.[3] These can be submitted by e-mail.

However, if the instructor is such a dinosaur as to wish to administer *graded tests*, the mechanics to construct online tests already exist on programs such as Moodle. (No one has yet discovered how to prevent cheating on such tests. The solution—using a method pioneered by Humpty-Dumpty in *Through the Looking-Glass*—is to redefine the word. "Cheating" can become "collaborative learning," "group assessment," "research-based testing," or some other comforting euphemism.)

ATHLETICS

Obviously it will not be possible for a NORBS to field sports teams in any traditional sense. However, as it is absolutely unthinkable for any American high school not to have a competitive athletics component—indeed, such a lack could result in loss of accreditation if not charges of treason to the founding ideals of the Republic—we will enable our students to compete with other schools via video games. It will surely be possible to organize teams to play various sports using online games, and we can perhaps expand into nontraditional sports including MMORPGs and other over-the-airwaves competitions. Properly managed, they should offer as many chances for self-aggrandizement, bragging, inflated egos,

17

misplaced priorities, and enabling parents to live vicariously through their children, as do traditional sports.

Basic physical fitness—which certainly *is* important—will be maintained by students running in place and doing pushups and jumping jacks in front of their webcams, supervised by "coaches" wearing T-shirts, with whistles around their necks.

OTHER MATTERS

Students will have ninety minutes of Evening Study Hall, Sunday through Thursday, monitored over a webcam by that day's duty master.

At lights-out the school will ring a virtual bell on all cell phones to tell students to go to bed. Parents will have to be responsible for seeing that their children stay in bed and rise on time.

Parents will also have to feed their kids; but the school will send out menu suggestions weekly so that, in theory anyway, the student body can be offered identical food.

At Graduation, the seniors will sit in cap and gown before their computers so they can, like their contemporaries, listen to music by Edward Elgar, receive edifying advice from a commencement speaker, benefit from the Headmaster's closing remarks, and hear their names called. Seniors will be e-mailed diplomas, which they can print out.

CONCLUSION

This pioneering essay has, of course, many lacunae, but readers cannot expect every loose end to be tied up in a few pages. Using this as a basis, others will fill in the blanks and proceed with the bold experiment. Surely the chance to offer to the public all the benefits of a college preparatory boarding school experience at a fraction of the cost of traditional on-campus education[4] and minimal infrastructure means this seminal essay will not lack supporters!

----

[1] A fictional account of this consultant's message—but, unfortunately, not nearly as fictional as I wish it were—may be found in Chapters 5, 25, and 36 of my novel *And Gladly Teach*.

[2] Throughout this monograph I am using generic terms when referring to technological devices. Since it is hardly worth a grown man's time to try keeping up with the proliferation of neologisms for computers, cell phones, hand-held devices, etc.—for all I know, the cell phone is by now called a celone and the hand-held computer a haheco—the more knowledgeable reader should simply substitute for my generic term the correct name of whatever meretricious gewgaw occupies this week's headlines.

[3] I hope nobody expects me to define this verbiage. I do not know what most of these terms mean. I merely copied them from a memo sent out by a particularly progressive colleague earlier this year, confident that they embody cutting-edge pedagogy and the wave of the future.

[4] A fraction of cost *to the school* is meant. Tuition will be kept in the $30,000 range.

8. ON INSTITUTIONAL ADVANCEMENT

Let us imagine that you find a family living in a dilapidated old house. The roof leaks; the windows are cracked; the carpets are threadbare; the furnace is erratic, often providing much heat in warm weather and little heat when it is cold. The stone walls are crumbling.

Let us also imagine that you—Mr. Hastings van Rensselaer Plutocrat— are wealthy and altruistic. You wish to assist this family. You leave your mansion in Palm Desert, California, and go to them. You smilingly announce that you are going to help them. You will construct in their yard a fine marble fountain that will send a beautiful spray of water fifty feet into the air; further, you will hang upon their living room wall— over the cracks—a genuine Gobelin tapestry depicting colorful scenes of medieval pageantry.

In proper recognition of your generosity a fine bronze plaque will be affixed to the fountain designating it the Plutocrat Water Display and the tapestry will appropriately bear a small label "Gift of H. van R. Plutocrat, 2013." Your benevolence will be fittingly acknowledged at a public ceremony where you will be hailed as a modern Maecenas, a philanthropist extraordinaire.

How happy this family will surely be! Even as they sit in their cold, drafty living room watching the rain drip into the buckets placed under the holes in the roof, they will hardly be able to stifle their cries of joy as they admire the intricate weaving of the tapestry and marvel at the loveliness of the fountain.

If this seems like an absurd flight of fancy, I have to suggest that, unfortunately, it is not. It is analogous to what can happen when a combination of generosity, self-esteem, and misplaced priorities, facilitated by faulty fund-raising policies, are brought to bear on an impoverished institution—such as, to choose a random example, a tuition-driven boarding school.

Would it not make more sense, if, before adorning a shack with golden gables, one first repaired the walls? If the roof leaks, should the construction of a magnificent garage be the first priority? When the heating system is antique and undependable, one might replace it before installing a jacuzzi, might one not? Should one not water the lily before gilding it?

Surely it does not strain credulity to assert that institutional advancement implies that the institution must have a sound infrastructure before more buildings are built and comparative frills added. That is common sense. Why then is it not done?

One reason may be that some potential philanthropists feel that to endow a grand building, to construct a statue, to equip rooms with huge tables that the users of those rooms neither want nor need, is preferable to repairing a heating system or tuck-pointing a crumbling wall, because building, constructing, and equipping offer more opportunities for recognition than repairing and replacing. Perhaps such people feel that little prestige attaches to renovating bathrooms or laying carpets, to fixing roofs or caulking windows. After all, the pharaohs are remembered for pyramids, not for cottages.

I suggest that it is the function of Development Departments not to take the easy way out by abetting such erroneous notions and soliciting money for secondary things, but to grasp the nettle and tell potential donors what is really needed. If Lorenzo the Magnificent, class of '53, announces he will finance an air-conditioned, twenty-lane bowling alley, it is the job of the Institutional Advancement experts to tell him (politely but firmly) that the institution does not need such a thing, but does need—to invent an exaggerated, unlikely example—to prevent a dormitory that has visible cracks in its outer walls and whose windows are out of plumb from continuing its slow but steady descent into a ravine, so would he kindly write a check for these much-needed repairs to an already-existing structure even though it is not named after him?
So, wealthy, public-spirited alumni: when your alma mater needs shoes and a dress, do not give her a feather boa. When she huddles in the cold, do not give her a painting of a fireplace. When her house is falling down, do not offer to build her a tanning salon next door.

And advancement officials: take the bull by the horns and insist that you have a strong, well-built cart before you get a horse, or a white elephant, to pull it. Repair the infrastructure before adding to the superstructure.

For if this is not done, the eventual fate of institutions which do not do it might well be that so famously depicted by Shelley:

21

I met a traveller from an antique land

Who said, "Two vast and trunkless legs of stone

Stand in the desert. Near them, on the sand,

Half-sunk, a shattered visage lies….

And on the pedestal these words appear --

'My name is Ozymandias, king of kings:

Look on my works, ye Mighty, and despair!'

Nothing beside remains. Round the decay

Of that colossal wreck, boundless and bare,

The lone and level sands stretch far away."

    Maybe Ozymandias built an Arts Center when he really should have repaired his palace.

9. *from* THE FACULTY LOUNGE - A GUIDE

.... On either hand stand two machines. These are multi-purpose copiers—i.e. they can malfunction in many different ways. When they do this, a sort of alphabet soup of letters and lines lights up on their control panels, inaugurating yet another Quest for the Concealed Stationery, an exciting event in which adventurers search for all the out-of-the-way spots that a photocopier can hide, fold, spindle, and mutilate sheets of paper. The cries of delight that questers give as each sheet, or fragment, is exhumed; the discovery, even by veteran adventurers, of yet another crevice, niche, or oubliette where these crafty machines can secrete a page; the gentle mockery of the lettered lights announcing that, despite heroic efforts on your knees, you have still not yet found area A2; the anxiety of trying to get tests printed as the seconds tick by to the class bell: all these are part of the enjoyment provided at no extra charge. (Rumor has it that if a machine jams so completely that all the lights go on at once, you win the grand prize and coins will cascade from a slot.)

Particularly heroic adventurers have been known to try to make two-sided copies, or even transparencies. People with high blood pressure should not attempt this.

*

The furnishings and decor of the Lounge were obviously chosen with great care, not only individually but for ensemble effect. You have perhaps heard of *feng shui*, the Chinese art of orienting and arranging a space and its contents to achieve maximum serenity. The Faculty Lounge was laid out according to a lesser-known North Korean doctrine called *ick poo*, the art of orienting and arranging a space and its contents so as to drive everyone out in the shortest possible time and induce an abhorrence of ever coming back. The Lounge has been rightly hailed as a paragon of *ick poo*, rivaling if not surpassing North Korea itself.

For example, a tiny refrigerator stands against the southern wall. It contains nothing edible. This is just as well, because the *ick poo* experts put the refrigerator not three feet from the main radiator. But this minuscule fridge is further from the radiators than are the bottles of water used to supply the Culligan cooler near the windows....

10. EVELYN WAUGH ON EDUCATIONAL REFORM

I read *Scott-King's Modern Europe* (published in 1947) many years ago. The last paragraphs impressed me then; more recently they have impressed me even more. In fact I am tempted to have them embossed on a great banner that I can hang on my classroom door.

Mr. Scott-King, a fusty Latin teacher at an old English public school, returns from an excursion that has taken him, much against his will, to a European dictatorship and a Palestinian refugee camp (from which he was rescued by a former student). The Headmaster tries to persuade him to teach something more 'useful' than Latin, since the number of Latinists at the school is dwindling.

"You know," the Headmaster said, "we are starting this year with fifteen fewer classical applicants than we had last term."

"I thought that would be about the number."

"I deplore it as much as you do. But what are we to do? Parents are not interested in producing the 'complete man' any more. They want to qualify their boys for jobs in the modern world. You can hardly blame them, can you?"

"Oh yes," said Scott-King. "I can and do. I think it would be very wicked indeed to do anything to fit a boy for the modern world."

"It's a shortsighted view, Scott-King."

"There, Headmaster, with all respect, I differ from you profoundly. I think it is the most long-sighted view it is possible to take."

11. HEALTHY EATING

As part of its sedulous concern for the welfare of its workers, my school favors us with periodic health tips via a newsletter—the *Wellness Weekly*—published by a benevolent organization. The issues that came out just before the holiday season offered advice on how one should approach that dangerous time—a time that the writers of the newsletter apparently assume to be a period of gluttony, self-indulgence, and sybaritic abandon that would make the Roman Saturnalia look like a Quaker prayer meeting—without entirely destroying one's constitution.

Of course, this is not the first time I have seen such helpful screeds. One can hardly go on the Internet or enter a store without finding signs, handouts, and flyers that proffer advice, monitions, and scary predictions concerning the consequences of eating food—almost any food. Merely reading the many articles that appear in the News section of Yahoo.com could convince a person that hardly anything is safe.

I have concluded that the basic belief held by the authors of these manifestos is that all food is poison and that it would be far better if we could eat nothing at all, or at least nothing that tasted good or in any way appealed to human beings.

But since. alas, human beings do have to eat, the dietary experts have undertaken to make us feel as guilty as possible about it, so we will eat as little as possible. Their language is remarkable. We are told we may "allow" ourselves a cookie at a Christmas party; that we should eat some "healthy" concoction before going out so as to minimize our evil lust to consume a sausage or a brownie later on; that we ought to seek out the plate of broccoli and celery while fighting down the death-wish—a wish perhaps the result of the inherent wickedness imparted by Original Sin—to instead have a fried onion ring. The day after we blaspheme the temple of our body by riotous gourmandizing we must, of course, head for the gym and exercise especially hard so as to exorcise the aftereffects of insensate indulgence.

The language of these publications really is a bit theological. We are prone to sin—sin in this case that may result in crippling ourselves and bringing pain and misery to our loved ones when we collapse as a result of easily-avoided dietary wickedness—and must seek forgiveness by, for example, a few hours on a treadmill. (Did you know that treadmills were used as punishment in Victorian-era prisons? Yes. Prisoners were compelled to put in so many hours on a treadmill. Think how healthy they were at the end of their sentences. And they didn't even have to pay for using the equipment!)

As one who was brought up in the pre-Vatican II Catholic Church, I can speak with some authority on techniques of inducing guilt: the modern food-haters are doing a good job. I am sure they have succeeded in removing joy from the lives of many people. Even at a holiday party we cannot eat an hors-d'oeuvre without a premonition of doom; as you pop that small, wizened sausage into your mouth you can feel a stain spreading onto your soul; you find yourself excusing your reckless indulgence in a handful of popcorn by resolving to starve yourself for a week to make up for your transgression. This is an improvement on the Confessional: the sinner now assigns himself his own penance even as he commits the sin.

I do not think the heralds of health go far enough, however. So I would like to offer a few ideas on how each of us can contribute to the welfare of our fellow men:

1) If you are invited to, let us say, a New Year's party, station yourself next to the table that bears the most seductive goodies. Be sure to have with you a heavy ruler and a bag of healthy food. Whenever some libertine is about to pick up a cheese cracker, rap him sharply on the knuckles with the ruler and offer him a carrot. Recalled as by a guardian angel from impending corruption by a Satanic canapé, he will surely be grateful.

2) Bring with you to parties pictures of malnourished children. (You can easily print these from the Internet.) Scatter them about the snack tables. This should induce healthy guilt into all the revelers.

3) Cards printed with improving slogans such as these can be placed at strategic spots:

- A moment on the lips, but a lifetime on the hips.

- A slice of cake and you're at your wake.

- "Devil's-Food" indeed!

- An apple tart may stop your heart.

- Abandon all hope, ye who nibble here!

- Like some pie? Prepare to die.

- The way to Hell is paved with chocolate cupcakes.

- *Water* is *God's* champagne.

The health savants, as well as the spirits of Oliver Cromwell, John Calvin, and all our Puritan forebears, will surely thank you (even if no one else does).

12. MORE HEALTH

The latest issue of the *Wellness Weekly* arrived today and after reading it I saw that I need not cudgel my brains to come up with funny stuff, I need only reprint the newsletter verbatim. I suppose that doing that might cause copyright problems, though, so today I offer just one item from the Weekly, from the article "Top 10 Ways to Control Portions":

5. **Keep seconds out of sight**: Don't serve family meals family-style. Keep pots and dishes away from the table where it's all too easy to go for seconds. If the extra food is right in front of you, you are more likely to continue to eat than if you had to get up from the table to have seconds.

Now perhaps you think I made that up. But I did not. It's right in front of me in black and white. "Don't serve family meals family-style." Someone really wrote that and did not see either humor or irony.

I would like to offer a suggestion to the publisher of the *Wellness Weekly*: why stop at half measures? Here is a revised version:

5. **Hide the food**. After slaving for hours to prepare a delicious meal, place minuscule portions of each item on tiny plates, then hide the rest in the attic. If any diners are so wicked and greedy as to wish to eat more of your food, tell them to go get it. After climbing a couple of flights of stairs, getting cobwebs in their hair, and banging their heads on the rafters, perhaps the insatiable gluttons will think twice about gorging themselves. After all, what better compliment can there be for a cook than for people not to eat her food? After the meal, go to the attic, get the extra food, and throw it away. That's the best thing, after all—nasty, evil food. Poison, all of it.

PS – Did you know that "3 oz. of meat is the size of a deck of cards, 1 oz. of meat is the size of a matchbook, and 1 cup of potatoes, rice, or pasta looks like a tennis ball"? That's item number 9 in this week's bulletin. Careful diners will of course want to carry a deck of cards, a matchbook, and a tennis ball with them whenever they succumb to the temptation to eat, so they will not accidentally eat 4 oz. of meat or 1½ cups of rice.

13. YET MORE HEALTH

1) From the March issue of *Consumer Reports OnHealth*: "An English study found that women who took a brisk 15-minute walk reduced their desire for chocolate…. All of the groups reported a lower level of craving—and were less tempted by images of chocolate…"

I assume that the value of this English study is to warn women against taking 15-minute walks and thus depriving themselves of enjoying one of the most delicious and nutritious foods on our planet, one of the things that makes our wretched existence bearable.

2) In the March issue of *Consumer Reports* there is a review called "Top Popcorns." It begins thus: "Plenty of Americans reach for popcorn when it's time to watch the Oscars, the Crawleys, or the latest zombie attack. When we asked readers their favorite snack during special shows, popcorn led the list. (To our readers' credit, 'Nothing: I don't snack' came in second.)"

You see? You see what these people are doing to us? In an article that reviews popcorn, the writers *commend* those (16.7%) who never touch it—who, indeed, "don't snack." In an article that tells you which popcorn is best to eat, we are made to feel guilty about eating it. How frail and wicked we are! How we must admire the stalwart Puritans who never snack, who sit there nobly not enjoying a light collation of goodies, who resist the promptings of Satan to eat between meals. (And God knows what their meals consist of. Probably celery sticks and clear broth.)

The same issue of CR contains a long article about the best TV sets to buy. It might be better if the magazine warned people about wasting their time watching the Oscars, the Crawleys (whoever they may be), or zombie attacks.

14. JUST WHAT THE DOCTOR ORDERED

One goes to the emergency room for succor in adversity: a nascent kidney stone, perhaps; pain in one's extremities or bowels. One is treated kindly, examined, tested, reassured, and dispatched to a pharmacy with appropriate prescriptions for the alleviation of anguish and infection.

Like the people we see on those notices in the post office, medicines go about under many names, and one wonders if pharmaceutical companies are staffed by people who write Heroic Fantasy in their spare time. ("When the tyrant Ketorolac sent his armies, under his ferocious vizier Meloxicam, to plunder the peaceful kingdom of Ativan, only the hero Celebrex, wielding the enchanted sword Lorazepam, stood between his people and subjection to the evil Flurbiprofen Empire...")

Pharmacists now need printers as well as pestles, for, along with the cute little orange storage jars in which pills and powders are dispensed, one receives also a page – two pages – several pages – of information on each medicament.

If one takes time to read these screeds—not always an easy matter, as some are printed in 6- or 8-point type—one may well decide to live with one's pain and misery rather than risk the utter destruction that may follow if you dare to swallow one of those pills.

Here is a capsule to "relieve pain and swelling... treat headaches, backaches, tendonitis..., gout." A worthy goal. But... but... "NSAID medicines may increase the chance of a heart attack or stroke that can lead to death." "Serious side effects include: heart failure from body swelling; life-threatening skin reactions; liver problems including liver failure;" and six other things. Some are less serious: "Possible Side Effects... include upset stomach, nausea, vomiting, heartburn, gas, headache, diarrhea, constipation, drowsiness, or dizziness." "Contact Your Doctor Immediately," it says, "if they continue or are bothersome." (*If*!? Are vomiting, etc. not "bothersome" to some people (Spartans, Stoics, masochists?))

You read these pages, nervously moisten your lips, and inspect the medicine jar. No, it doesn't say Dr. Lucrezia Borgia. But look here... "Possible Side Effects" for another medication you were given to take along with the first one: "blue or purple skin color, yellowing of the skin or eyes..." "Check with your doctor as soon as possible" it adds helpfully: valuable advice indeed, as many might otherwise not think to do that for a trifle like turning purple.

Perhaps there is something to be said for illiteracy, or for just not reading these information sheets. After all, the basic instructions are on the label, e.g. *Aqua Tofana: take one every four hours.* Ignorance is bliss. Che sarà, sarà. Trust the doctor, be a man, take the pills and go about your business. Yes. Indeed. But... if you take Phenozopyrid (alias Pyridium, a.k.a. Phenazopyridine) without reading about it, and then use the toilet, you will suddenly discover that the water in the bowl becomes orange: vivid, almost neon, orange. Then you will wish, after you recover from your faint, that you *had* read "This medicine may cause the urine to turn orange or red. This is harmless but it may stain fabric." And you will have similar feelings if your soft contact lenses turn orange because you wore them while taking Pyridium.

There is much other helpful advice. "Check with your doctor as soon as possible if you experience memory loss." Hmmm, yes... now what was it I was going to do after I took that pill? "If overdose is suspected, contact your poison control center or emergency room immediately. Symptoms of overdose may include confusion, slow reflexes, clumsiness, deep sleep, and loss of consciousness." Perhaps your unconscious self can make the call.

"Check with your doctor"—this mantra is incessant. Pharmaceutical companies seem to use it as a safety valve to excuse their inability to abolish potentially catastrophic side effects. Do they expect doctors to set aside a couple of hours a day to deal with patients who are swelling up or turning purple?

People who live alone, at least, might well decide to take their nostrums only where help is at hand: at parties or the theater, in church, or... why not right in the lobby of the emergency room? Just pop in two or three times a day with a glass of water, gulp down your pills, and sit there shuddering quietly, waiting to see if the Sword of Damocles will descend this time.

And now one can see why, along with Phenazopyridine and Naproxen, one was given Lorazepam ("a benzodiazepine used to relieve anxiety..."): If you had no anxiety before you went to the e.r., you will most certainly have it once you have read about your medicine.

"DO NOT EXCEED THE RECOMMENDED DOSE" it says emphatically on all the sheets. No fear. The challenge is nerving oneself to take the minimum dose.

Now, if you'll excuse me, I have to go fill prescriptions for Mortufax and Thanatophilin. I hope they have no bothersome side effects.

31

15. HISTORICAL FILMS

Here, arranged chronologically, is a list of historical—some even historic—movies that I think well worth seeing, followed by a few that are less valuable. Given my interests and training, most of these films are about war or European politics.

I am not pedantic in judging the historical value of a film. I know that any treatment of a historical topic has to compress and simplify. I do not get upset if there are too few buttons on a uniform or if one character is used to represent several. But I do get upset with falsehood and blatant distortion.

1) **Cleopatra**. This extravaganza almost bankrupted Fox and is perhaps best remembered today for the love affair between two of its stars, Taylor and Burton. But in fact the writers paid attention to history and tried to be accurate about Caesar, Antony, and the Serpent of the Nile. The sets are awesome. The two-hour special that comes with the film is very interesting, too.

2) **El Cid**. Another spectacular, and one that certainly simplifies the life of Rodrigo Diaz de Vivar—there is no reference to his many years of work as a mercenary for the Moors, for instance. But there is a nobility about the central character and his actions that is inspiring, and the last part has more relevance today than it did before 2001…

3) **Joan of Arc**. The 1948 film with Ingrid Bergman and Jose Ferrer, in which Ms. Bergman does a remarkable job in conveying the purity and nobility of la Pucelle. Very moving.

4) **The Taking of Power By Louis XIV**. An awkward title and a film that is far more talk than action; but Roberto Rossellini does a fine job of describing how and why the young Louis acted to control the nobles and make himself effective absolute king. The scenes (towards the end) of the king at dinner and at court are quite marvelously done. French with subtitles.

5) **Danton**. A study of the improvised nature of French government under the Terror, and of Robespierre and the title character. (If it began two years before it does it might have been called "The Losing of Power By Louis XVI" and been sold as a set with item 4.)

6) **The Alamo**. The 2004 film directed by J.L. Hancock. Although the interpretation of Santa Anna by Emilio Echevarria seems a bit over the top, the film tries to remain faithful to people and events in describing this heroic incident, the American Thermopylae.

7) **The Charge of the Light Brigade**. Not the Errol Flynn historical fiction opus but the 1968 film with Sir John Gielgud and David Hemmings. Aside from an inexplicable and completely dispensable theme involving Vanessa Redgrave as an unfaithful wife, this is a very good film about the early Victorian military and the famous mistaken attack.

8) **Gettysburg**. The film wisely concentrates on three events: the first day's fighting, the defense of Little Round Top by the 20th Maine, and of course Pickett's Charge. Yes, I know that Gen. Longstreet's beard looks wrong and that the first Confederate soldier you see is too fat, but don't get hung up on trivia. This is an excellent film.

9) **Gone With The Wind**. Of course this is fiction, based on a novel; but it certainly captures the life of the antebellum South (as lived by the tiny number of really wealthy planters), the horror of the war on the home front, and some of the difficulties of Reconstruction.

10) **Breaker Morant**. A great film about three Australians accused of atrocities during the nasty last phase of the Boer War. It makes you think.

11) **Nicholas and Alexandra**. This is an outstanding piece of history, compressing into a couple of hours many of the problems of Romanov Russia in its last days and the personalities of the last tsar and tsarina. And you'll remember Rasputin. Academy Award for costumes.

12) **Gandhi**. Although the personality of the title character is presented too worshipfully, the basic history is there and the sense of being in India is overwhelming (at least for viewers who, like me, have never been in India).

13) **Zulu**. The personalities and relationship of Lts. Chard and Bromhead (and of Rev. Witt) are fictionalized, but the story as a whole is true and exciting. And there will never be a better British RSM (in this case at company level) than Colour-Sergeant Bourne.

14) **A Night To Remember**. This is the *Titanic* film everyone should see, even if it *is* in black & white. No mawkish love story gets in the way of the real story. The Criterion Collection edition has very good commentary by two authorities on the ship.

15) **The Last Emperor**. A masterpiece. What a portrayal of an entirely different society than ours! See it.

16) **Lawrence Of Arabia**. I hardly have to recommend this, do I? While hazy on chronology—I wish they mentioned a few dates—it certainly captures the legendary essence of its eccentric subject.

17) **Oh What A Lovely War**. This musical is a good commentary on the War to End War.

18) **Tora, Tora, Tora**. This is almost a documentary study of the events leading to Pearl Harbor. A very fine film.

19) **Patton**. It's not really a war film—the battle scenes are its weakest part—but a psychological study of a complex, remarkable man.

20) **Valkyrie**. I did not think that modern Hollywood would do so good a job with the July 20 plot. But Tom Cruise did very well indeed. (I do not in the least mind the American accents.)

21) **Is Paris Burning?**. This vast film has been largely forgotten. It's a fair and balanced study of its subject from both the French and German viewpoints. Gert Frobe (Goldfinger) plays Gen. Choltitz, the Paris commandant. Black and white, unfortunately.

22) **A Bridge Too Far**. An hour too long, I think, and I have trouble accepting Elliott Gould as a colonel of infantry, but this epic captures the spirit and facts of Operation Market-Garden, especially the massive airborne drops and Col. Frost's heroic defense of the key bridge.

23) **Downfall**. Wow. This is the last word on "Hitler in the bunker." No further film treatment is ever necessary. Not a study only of the by-then-demented dictator, but of all the inmates of the bunker. A tremendous film. German, with subtitles.

1) **300**. The seniors in my Greece and Rome elective kept urging me to see this, although with giggles. (They knew enough about the subject to guess my reaction.) It falls into a category I especially dislike: a film that, by replacing ignorance with falsehood, leaves the general public knowing less about the subject than before seeing it. Certainly a rip-roaring gorefest, but otherwise … ick.

2) **Gladiator**. This thing won the Academy Award for Best Picture? *The Fall of the Roman Empire* (1964), of which this bloody (I use the word in both the sanguinary and British senses) film is essentially a remake, is much better. Much of this is violence masquerading as art.

3) **Braveheart**. This probably would have been a better film if Mel Gibson were not so intense an Anglophobe. It is largely fiction, and eventually becomes really silly (e.g. the amour between William Wallace and the Princess of Wales). Impressive battle scene, of course; but the Battle of Stirling Bridge was very different than what we see.

4) **Cromwell**. This film has scant historical value because the producers decided to portray the English Civil War as a personal confrontation between Charles I and Oliver Cromwell, which it was not. (For example, Cromwell never met the king, nor was he one of the five M.P.s whom Charles tried to arrest in 1642.) However, it is worth seeing because the battle scenes give a flavor of musket and pike warfare and because Alec Guinness gives a wonderful performance as Charles I, right down to the slight stammer, and the Scots burr that creeps in when he is agitated. The trial and execution scenes are very well done. The film also gives you a chance to see Albus Dumbledore and James Bond at early stages of their careers (Richard Harris plays Cromwell; Timothy Dalton plays Prince Rupert).

5) **Waterloo**. This film—unavailable on DVD for, I suppose, legal reasons—is hard for me to evaluate. The costumes are perfect. Since most of the Russian army was apparently made available for filming, there is no shortage of extras. The score is fine. Some scenes are excellent: the Emperor's farewell at Fontainebleau, the great cavalry charges (with the aerial shots so clearly showing the British squares), Orson Welles as Louis XVIII. I read that Rod Steiger decided to play

Napoleon as "a man needing a rest and a hot bath," which I guess is justifiable. But more should have been done with the Prussians (both at Ligny and on the 18th); Napoleon did not suffer some kind of seizure at the height of the battle; there was no hurricane near the end of the battle (I think someone accidentally turned on a wind machine); some scenes are incomplete, especially the charge of the Scots Greys (a charge that does not hit anything; there is no indication that much of d'Erlon's corps was rendered ineffective by the charge). I have heard that some hours of film are still available. Grognards like me can only hope that the entire available footage is eventually released.

6) **Gods and Generals**. The successor to *Gettysburg* and one of the biggest turkeys ever committed to celluloid. Long and boring. Why cover Fredericksburg instead of Antietam? Why spend so very much time on Stonewall Jackson? Seldom has so much effort, such attention to detail, been put into a more unsuccessful film—which shows that minute historical accuracy (e.g. Jackson being wounded in the finger at First Bull Run) does not guarantee a good movie. And what a pity, since its failure prevented the making of what would have been a trilogy.

16. STAR WARS I: THE PHANTOM MESS

The immortal main theme begins. The orange words appear: "Turmoil has engulfed the Galactic Republic. The taxation of trade routes to outlying systems is in dispute. Hoping to resolve the matter with a blockade of deadly battleships, the greedy Trade Federation has stopped all shipping to the small planet of Naboo.... This alarming chain of events..."

Do we sit in wonder, our popcorn halfway to our mouths, as chills run down our spines? Good lord! A *trade dispute*. A *blockade of a small planet*. A *chain of events* (albeit quite a small chain, with only two links).

This is the stuff of which epics are made?

What is the purpose of the blockade? Shouldn't the Trade Federation *want* to trade with Naboo? Perhaps the T.F. wants to charge higher prices? We never learn anything about the dispute, other than that it is legal and trivial. ("Something as trivial as this trade dispute," says Qui-Gon; "Our blockade is perfectly legal" says Viscount Gunray.) Since the plot opening is a legal, trivial trade dispute, we might expect the first exciting scene to be a committee hearing by economic experts.

How could Mr. Lucas give us so lackluster a start to so eagerly anticipated a movie?

*

Queen Amidala... yes. Now, his films demonstrate that Mr. Lucas's general knowledge of government and diplomacy is so minuscule that it could be engraved on the head of a pin with room left over, but in the polity of Naboo he has confected something particularly fascinating: a democratic monarchy, a queen who is elected and subject to term limits. This "queen" is required to wear preposterous costumes that change hourly and coiffures not seen since the court of Louis XVI. Surely she would have little time to do much governing, being too busy with her clothes and hair. But that might be a good idea, since the office of monarch apparently has no age qualification. In this crisis Naboo is governed by a girl of fourteen. That's the best the voters of Naboo could do? (And she, we are told in Film II, is not the youngest ever chosen. One would like to see the youngest, who perhaps ruled from a cradle rather than a throne.)

*

We arrive on Tatooine, where a serious difficulty arises: the hyperdrive is kaput. It is a matter of galactic importance that the ship get going ASAP. Only one dealer, Watto, an overgrown housefly, has the needed part, and he will not accept Republic currency.

What is a resourceful, masterful, intelligent Jedi to do? Here are some possibilities:

(A) Go to a bank and convert your money to the local stuff.

(B) Inform Watto that the Jedi Order is commandeering his hyperdrive and will wire him the money. If he refuses, take it by force.

(C) Do nothing until you accidentally discover that a small child might get you money by winning a race, although this child has never finished, let alone won, a race.

Guess what Qui-Gon does. We can only shake our heads.

A side note: Qui-Gon asks Obi-Wan if they have anything to trade with. He replies that they have little but "the queen's wardrobe". Folks, the queen's wardrobe could be traded for most of the starships on the planet.

*

Anakin's poor mother: here is the biggest, most glaring plot hole in the whole series. Why in heaven is she left as a slave? The Jedi are willing to take a nine-year-old boy away from his only parent and forget about her. There is never any effort to free her, not even after her son shows her a pile of cash and says, "Look how much we won." Apparently he keeps it and leaves mom to the mercy of the giant fly.

*

"Gungans go to sacred place." The Trade Federation has occupied the planet; they know about the underwater city. Yet thousands of not very inconspicuous or diminutive Gungans manage to move themselves and tons of military equipment to someplace on the surface that the T.F. never notices. How did they do that? But of course we must reckon with "Lucas logic" as well as "Star Wars physics". This also means that dei ex machinae can be produced as needed. Must you get into the city? Voilà, "the secret passage on the waterfall side." Thank heaven for secret passages. And how we rejoice when Padmé produces the necessary pistols from the arm of a chair in which Newt Gunray has sat for weeks without ever discovering the concealed weapons.

*

When the big metal door goes up and Darth Maul appears, the two Jedi say "we'll handle this" and the others—over a dozen armed men— just leave (to "take the long way," even though they are in a great hurry). Why doesn't everyone open fire and kill the Sith right there?

*

One could go on listing absurdities and inconsistencies in this silly movie, but enough of examples. It is more important to ask why. Why is this film so badly written? Why are thoughtful viewers left feeling cheated?

I think the answer can be found on the commentary track, where Mr. Lucas and several mechanics talk to us.

My impression is of men so mesmerized by technology that they have lost sight of what really matters. These animators and CGI people—these hod-carriers of the movie world—are insufferable. On and on they go with details of how this or that shot was done, repeatedly telling us of their cleverness, their expertise, their great deeds. One feels a bit "wude" in saying this, but, folks, *we don't care* how it's done. You are but hewers of imaginary wood and drawers of virtual water. Do your jobs, cash your paychecks, and be quiet. We, the audience, care only about the finished product. Save your war stories for others in your skilled trade. You deserve well of your master, undoubtedly other computerists will want to know the details of your craft, but don't monopolize the commentary with one more description of how you created realistic-looking dust or inserted a suitable wobble into a puppet. Sheesh!

Mr. Lucas's comments suggest he is an overgrown adolescent. One hopes in vain for some insight on such things as the government system of Naboo or what reaction he expected from the startling announcement of Anakin's virgin birth (made before we hear of the midi-chlorians). What he most often says--over and over, in all three films—is how much more he can do with CGI today than a few years ago. Incessantly he rejoices that he can now, at last, bring his ideas to life. But what ideas? Not moving or dramatic ones—just glitz. He often compares his work to that of a composer, referring again and again to "tone poems" and suchlike. I can only suggest that, if he thinks his films are like music, he should have let John Williams do the directing as well as the composing. The result would have been superior. As it is, *The Phantom Menace*, in its full absurd, inconsistent, ridiculous glory, is useful mainly as proof that Mr. Lucas can no longer invent a coherent plot, write a decent script, or make a film that can be taken seriously. He is now merely a master of eye-candy, of the colorful cinematic façade with emptiness behind it.

*

Finally, a tribute to Jar-Jar Binks. I am not being perverse. I like him. He brings to the film some much-needed humor. He does not take himself too seriously. He is genuine. He is humble. He is grateful. He helps his friends as best he can. I bet *he* wouldn't leave his mother in slavery. As for his language, I find it more refreshing and alive than that of a certain character who for no apparent reason always backwards speaks, whose verbs at the end of his sentences puts, and who so insufferably smug is that I almost wish Count Dooku his little green head had off cut.

STAR WARS II: TACKY CLOWNS

This weak film features several very large plot holes. The most obvious is the inability of the Jedi Order to see Anakin Skywalker's unfitness for his job.

Anakin is a precocious boy with little discipline. He is a hothead, a loose cannon, and emotionally involved with Padmé. He is not yet a good Jedi. But the Jedi Council—that collection of oh-so-sapient magi presided over by the Green Guru—ignores Obi-Wan's explicit warning and sends Anakin to guard Padmé. ("The Council is confident in its decision.")

A major source of Anakin's anxiety is his mother. This problem could of course have been solved if it had occurred to anyone to bring her to Coruscant, but nobody cares about poor Shmi. Even her loving son, with all his powers, is unable to come up with such a brainstorm as setting her free. And how limited communications seem to be in the galaxy: there have been no messages between Anakin and his mother for years. One might think she would drop him a line occasionally—at least a postcard, if she can't afford a hologram—to mention little things like her marriage. *He* might even try to write to *her*.

*

Obi-Wan and Anakin go to tremendous lengths to run down Zam, the assassin. When Zam is killed, however, and the two Jedi see the killer take off via rocket-pack, they just sit there looking at the dart. Why not chase *him*?

*

The diner scene is what Mr. Lucas calls a "homage to *American Graffiti*," but it is still idiotic. The resources of the Galactic Republic cannot discover where a dart comes from, but a short-order cook can (a cook who of course prospected "on Subterrel beyond the Rim", but apparently without much success considering the job he now has). And how humble of Mr. Lucas to pay homage to himself.

*

Among all the silly fairy-tale creatures with which Mr. Lucas populates his universe, the Kaminians take the cake. These effeminate giraffes hardly seem tough enough to run a war college, and they are so dumb they cannot see that Obi-Wan has not been sent to collect the clone army but is an intruder. (Jango Fett deduces this instantly.) Given such stupidity, one wonders how the Kaminians have managed to clone humans. But they are very generous in granting credit to customers: they have never written anyone about the 1,200,000 clones they think the Jedi

41

ordered; instead, they wait years for someone to show up and ask how things are going. (And who is paying for all this? Who's writing checks to Kamino? Why don't the Jedi try to find out?) The plot holes gape like canyons.

*

The comment track reinforces what I said before. The mechanics again bloviate on how clever they are. See how Sebulba's tentacles move! Behold him walking on his hands! Lo! Lama Su brushes his knee! ("An extra level of acting and realism" says the commentator. Really.) And the sound effects man is at least as annoying. Who cares how he produces noises?

*

The weirdest scene in any of the films is Scene 23 in this one. Senator ex-Queen Amadala—who, we recall, is five years Anakin's senior—tells her young admirer they cannot fall in love. (As Mr. Lucas mellifluously says in the commentary, "She's obviously older and, and, you know, in a professional thing that a queen, a senator, a leader so that she's much more reality-based in all of this…").

When giving Anakin her frigid message, Ms. Amidala chooses to wear a strapless black leather bustier and shoulder-high gloves, and to meet the ardent youth on a comfy sofa in a richly-furnished darkened room with a cozy fire burning on the hearth.

If this film had any depth, one would assume that the senator is actually trying to seduce Anakin, saying no with words but yes in every other way—or that she is setting him up for an assault charge when the overheated teenager jumps on her.

But because the film has no depth, we may infer that this scene is a dollop of cheesecake served up to the long-suffering daddies accompanying their tots to this kiddie flick—a motif repeated at the end of the film, when Ms. Portman, wearing a body stocking, has her costume lacerated by a big ugly monster, exposing her cute midriff, after which her bosom gets unaccountably bosomier in subsequent scenes until she is very bouncy indeed at 130:26. The commentary track, usually so loquacious about such matters, does not specify if this involved the use of CGI, although the effect is certainly more diverting than watching Lama Su brush his knee. (The reader will understand my attention to such details is evidence only of rigorous scholarship in the cause of cinematic criticism.)

*

So farewell to Star Wars II, another testimony to Mr. Lucas's inability to write any more decent or logical scripts, to the poverty of his mind, to

42

the victory of appearance over substance. But let us close with a game. I was hoping to see, among all the wondrous machines shown on the bonus disk, the Alphabet Soup Generator that picks character names. From the list below, pick the memorable names of real characters from among the silly names I made up.

1- Fangor Pondictat   5 - Depa Billaba   9 - Ask Aak

2 - Cronash Tal-Avarin   6 - Pooja Naberrie 10 - Elan Sleazebaggano

3 - Figraz Kloongarth   7 - Sio Bibble   11 – Yarael Poof

4 - Oppo Rancisis   8 - Plo Koon   12 - Triz Estonna

Answer: Nos. 1, 2, 3, and 12 are mine. The others were confected by Mr. Lucas.

STAR WARS III - REVENGE OF THE PLOT

Unlike films I and II, III has at least a clear story line. Mr. Lucas had to accomplish certain definite things to link with IV, so he could spend less time on tangents. But with advances in CGI and SFX, this one is even more dependent on mere visual glitter than the first: the opening battle is a good example. Alas, Mr. Lucas and his coterie of animators and computer mavens have been seduced by the dark... I mean, have reached the point where in their minds flashy things on the screen are a desirable substitute for story and acting.

The commentary is taken up by the usual technicians putting on airs, telling us how ingenious they are, preening themselves on their mastery of the "cutting edge" techniques of making movies without sets (or actors). Look, you rude mechanicals, what you are doing is making *cartoons*. People have been making cartoons since the 1930s. Your cartoons are technologically more sophisticated than, say, *Rocky and Bullwinkle*, but not inherently more moving or entertaining. Get over yourselves, computer boys. We do not stand in awe of your creations because in making them you used some shiny new thingamajig. Illogic, nonsense, plot holes a mile wide, glitz for the sake of glitz, do not become great because they are confected on blue screens. You would be doing more service to movies by reminding Mr. Lucas of this fact than by praising to the skies his every idea and enabling his increasing dependence on whiz-bangs to cover up his lack of substance.

*

My chief objections concern the end of the film.

Anakin joins the Sith primarily to save Padmé from death. But Palpatine finally tells him that this can be done only with additional research. ("If we work together, I know we can discover the secret.") But Padmé is to die in childbirth and is nine months pregnant, so it does not seem that there is much time to do this research, does it? Anakin should at this point have realized that Palpatine can do nothing to save his wife, and has been lying to him.

Padmé's death is entirely unconvincing. She is in good health. She is conscious and rational: she names her children. Then she dies. Why? Of a broken heart? Would not her maternal desire to raise two healthy children keep her alive? Would she die and abandon them? The real cause of Padmé's death is the plot: Mr. Lucas has to get rid of her because she never appears in IV - VI (except for Leia's now-obsolete comment that she remembers her mother, which is impossible). Surely our great *auteur* could have come up with a more convincing way to dispose of her.

"Hidden, safe, the children must be kept," says guess who. Yes, fine. How shall we do this? Let's give the girl to Bail Organa, one of the most conspicuous senators. No one will notice her then. As for the boy: "to Tatooine and his family send him." That will fool the Emperor and Darth Vader—they'd never think to look there, would they?

*

A comment on the sets of all the films: I am not the first to suggest that they are unrealistic. That is to say, every space looks so new, so neat, so frigid, that it is difficult to consider it real. The epitome of this fault is Anakin and Padmé's apartment. No one could think that human beings lived in that antiseptic mausoleum. What compulsion makes Mr. Lucas insist on sets looking so bleak, so sterile, so inhuman?

*

Mr. Lucas should have hired a writer—several writers. He no longer has the imagination and skill to write good scripts, so much so that sometimes the dialogue is sheer nonsense or non sequiturs. (Padmé's double says, as she dies, "I've failed you, senator" when in fact she has done exactly what she was supposed to. Newt Gunray tells Count Dooku he won't sign the treaty until Padmé is dead; a minute later Dooku says, with Gunray looking on, "Our friends in the Trade Federation have pledged their support." Lucas is interested not in sense but in spectacle (and marketing. Several times I almost wrote Lucre instead of Lucas.) He has been seduced by... oops, there I go again.

One last, finicky note: I wish that Obi-Wan Kenobi did not look like Tsar Nicholas II. It is disturbing for any historians who happen to watch the film.

***

It would be churlish, after this philippic, not to commend Mr. Lucas for Star Wars IV. *A New Hope* is a masterpiece. Mr. Lucas was inspired in his plotting and characters, and tireless in making the film in spite of many difficulties. He created a world we all love to visit and heroes we love to root for. Bravo!

*

Perhaps Mr. Lucas started so very well that there was no way to go but down. (Did he sense this before making Episode V (which he neither directed nor wrote the screenplay for) and Episode VI (directed, and partially written, by others)? Maybe, like Harper Lee in literature or Leoncavallo and Mascagni in music, he had just one great work in him. Maybe the crude state of Special Effects helped him: he could not use his glitzmeisters to cloud the screen with mere spectacle and was thus forced to depend more on his talent and wits, which atrophied as

45

it became easier to cover up poor plot and characters with bigger and bigger explosions.

How are the mighty fallen!

17.   THE CHOICES OF MASTER PETER

Peter Jackson's rendition of J.R.R. Tolkien's books has won so many awards that criticism might seem pointless, but criticize it I will, for I believe that Mr. Jackson's three movies (Special Extended Edition) are a betrayal of Tolkien's plot and characters and that it would have been better if the films had never been made because their success will make it difficult or impossible for anyone to get the chance to do a good job.

That the films are visually impressive no one can deny. We must commend the craftsmen who did so masterful a job with photography, costumes, and sets. The Weta Workshop is superb. The stunt team is magnificent. The attention to detail, the thought, the hard work that went into recreating Middle Earth, are wonderful. The opening of *Fellowship* is a fine interpretation of the Shire; I was enthralled to see what I had so often imagined as I read the books. Mr. Jackson deserves much praise for bringing together the master craftsmen and artisans he worked with, and no one can but admire his energy and organizing ability in making three huge films at once.

Unfortunately, the talented director evidently thinks he is also a talented writer, so this technical ability produced a deformed variant of Tolkien's novel. One might say it is as though a skilled craftsman, given the score of a Beethoven sonata, carefully built a magnificent piano, and then, fancying himself a composer as well as a builder, tinkered with the score and turned it into "Chopsticks".

Let us catalog a few of the cinematic crimes of PJ.

Frodo, instead of growing in wisdom and courage, remains a scared, clumsy, rather negligible pygmy who succeeds almost against his will. The worst betrayal of Tolkien in the films comes in *Fellowship*, when Arwen shows up to rescue the wounded Frodo. Setting aside the preposterous notion of Arwen as an Amazonian elf-maiden—an idiotic change—this means that Frodo is carried across the river like a sack of potatoes. His splendid defiance of the Black Riders ("By Elbereth and Luthien the Fair, you shall have neither the Ring nor me!") is replaced by some words written for Arwen; instead of growing, rising in our esteem, Frodo remains literally inert. This is the epitome of stupidity; it suggests that Mr. Jackson was unable to understand the books when he read them (insofar as he did: on ROTK Disc 2 (Scene 62) he says, "... because I

47

haven't obviously picked up the book and actually read the book for years. I've read little bits and pieces of it.... You lose the experience of the books as a whole and... I now... my mind is so muddled as to which is what" [i.e., he does not know how his movie differs from the book]).

As we go on, we see Frodo falling down a lot and opening his eyes very wide. Those are his main talents: falling down and staring. He falls down on every possible occasion, including an especially splendid belly-flop into the Dead Marshes.

Mr. Jackson betrays Tolkien's Aragorn by completely changing his motivation. In the books, he is a hero who, after decades of preparation, is ready to claim his rightful throne. In the film, he is a moral coward who has abandoned his heritage, who has to be argued into accepting his destiny as Isildur's heir.

Saruman, instead of being the too-clever conniver who hopes to outwit Sauron, seize the ring, and become master of Middle Earth, is simply Sauron's willing tool.

Théoden, a kindly, venerable old man who regains his courage, is too young, and portrayed as a liverish grouch who usually looks as though his ulcer was bothering him.

Elrond makes Théoden seem cheery. His expression—a permanent scowl—suggests his diet must consist mainly of lemons. And did he have to look like an aging hippie?

(I was happy to find, after I wrote these lines on Elrond, the following comments by Mike Hopkins, the Supervising Sound Editor, on the commentary track (Scene 30, where Elrond gives the re-forged sword to Aragorn—a scene not in Tolkien, of course). Mr. Hopkins says wryly that Elrond has not yet gone over the sea because the other elves told him, "'You're not coming to the (expletive) Undying Lands with us, you (expletive) moaning bastard. You'd just bring us all down.' Look at him. He's so (expletive) depressing, isn't he? I mean all he talks about is *doom*; we're all gonna *die*. Give that man a valium, some prozac." Mr. Hopkins's pungent insights suggest that I am not the only one to sense that the Elrond depicted in the films is not exactly what a great Elf-lord ought to be.)

Gimli. Oh lord. Someone should have told Mr. Jackson—since evidently he could not grasp it by himself—that dwarves are not noted humorists, but are dignified and serious almost to a fault. Turning Gimli into a buffoon, a zany, a figure of fun, ruins the character and gives us a series of embarrassingly stupid jokes and allusions that make us wince again and again. Every time the camera focuses on Gimli, we dread what will come out of his mouth.

Almost everywhere you touch these films, after the first half hour of *Fellowship*, they ring false, they fail. Hardly anything has not been marred. Treebeard has to be tricked into fighting by Pippin; Denethor, with no reference to the palantir that has maddened him, is a lunatic set up for a preposterous end that deprives him of all dignity (the "flying fireball"); Boromir's noble death is ruined by having him get up and fight again and again (the "human pincushion"); Aragorn falls over a cliff to extract a few cheap emotions from his friends... There is no end of such rubbish. These things did not save time or simplify the plot. They were deliberate decisions by Mr. Jackson, a man whose childish mind fits him only for the making of penny-dreadful horror movies.

A last example: the siege of Minas Tirith. In the books, an epic of bravery and resolution, courage and victory; in the film, the siege is resolved by the arrival of an army of bluish ghosts (what someone called the "scrubbing-bubbles of death") that surges over all opposition after Gandalf's staff has been broken (!), Gondor's ineffective soldiers are cowering, and Théoden's cavalry largely trampled by elephants. Tolkien dismissed the dead army after it seized the corsair fleet; Jackson brings it to Minas Tirith and ruins the whole battle scene.

One could go on for many more pages, but that would be too sad a task. These movies are a cream pie thrown in Tolkien's face by a yahoo incapable of appreciating the work of a great author. The usefulness of the films is to show how superior literature is to cinema (a sentiment that I later found the screenplay writers share—see below). What the humble scholar did alone, with a pen, in his spare time, towers far above what was done by the Great Director with thousands of assistants and a budget of many millions.

Tolkien's work is immortal. Jackson's films are meretricious.

Long live the Master! Down with the Falsifier!

*

The commentary tracks, especially that of the three writers, are often amusing and instructive. Mr. Jackson, Ms. Walsh, and Ms. Boyens sometimes engage in recriminations as to who was responsible for this or that atrocity or make desperate attempts to furnish reasons why they corrupted this or that part of Tolkien's plot. Sometimes they admit that a scene "attracted a certain amount of criticism" from "purists." (I suppose they mean people who expected that the greatest scenes in the book might also appear in the movies.) Listen, for example, to their writhings at Scene 48 of *Two Towers* (when elves arrive at Helm's Deep). Also of great interest are Ms. Walsh's comments at the very end of Two Towers (at 1:53:50, buried in the end-credits, with the names of the prosthetics supervisors on the screen)—interesting because she maintains that films are inferior to books and that it is impossible for a movie to do justice to Tolkien. ("You can't really have anything that comes close to the depth of the books.... You can't really hope to satisfy people who adore this book with the movie.... Films are entertainments, they're just not going to give you the pleasure that a book can give you.") These are telling admissions. (Mr. Jackson says nothing; silence implies consent.) I would raise the question: then why did you folks make the films at all? Perhaps the task should have fallen to someone who believes that a good film can do justice to a novel? Or at least someone who would make the effort?

It is also quite funny—although not so intended—to hear a writer, or an actor, happily point out some scene where the film does correspond to the book, often accompanied by an inane comment about how "this should please the fans"—as though these "fans" were some group of exigent eccentrics who had from time to time to be propitiated before the writers could get on with their real job of mangling Tolkien. For example, Sam grasps Frodo's hand when he first sees him at Rivendell: What fidelity to the text! How ecstatic are the fans! As though such trivia matters, coming as it does right after Xena, I mean Arwen, has carried the moribund Frodo over the Bruinen and ruined his whole character development. They seem to think "the fans" will overlook such betrayals because, for example, the director gave the hobbits huge hairy feet. I firmly believe "the fans" would have happily seen the hobbits wearing rubber boots had they been spared such things as Legolas skateboarding down stairs or Gimli saying, "Nobody tosses the dwarf"!

Matthew 23:24. (Ye blind guides, which strain at a gnat and swallow a camel.)

*

Mr. Jackson's co-writers may not deserve to be tarred with the same brush that must be so heavily applied to him. Some of the comments suggest that the two feel embarrassed by at least some of his depredations. Here is an excerpt from the commentary as Éomer arrives to relieve Helm's Deep: (PB = Ms. Boyens; FW = Ms. Walsh; PJ = the Great Director)

PB: Another slight departure from the book, but one, which I note with great interest, nobody ever worries about.

PJ: 'Cause this is really Erkenbrand...
PB: ...and Éomer is always in Helm's Deep and fighting side by side....
FW: It's because we committed much bigger sins.
PB: I know... well...
PJ: That's the whole plan. You commit a few big crimes and it takes everyone's eye away from the small ones, like a clever little detour...
PB: We could do courses in criminal screenwriting.
FW: Crimes Against the Books
PB: Crimes Against the Books 101.

And here is a transcription of the commentary near the start of Disc 2 of ROTK, when the Corsairs of Umbar appear.

PJ: Don't really need the scene at all. [!]
PB: (enthusiastically) No, not at all.
FW: I think 'painful' is a good and apt description.
PJ comments on his pirate cameo; a woman laughs as the ghost army
    attacks the fleet.
PJ: What? (Laughter continues)
FW: Now that's the moment at which the film passed from being, you know, a fantasy movie into a Monty Python moment. (PB Laughs harder.) What the hell? Was that the most motley crew...
PJ: Nothing wrong with Monty Python, though.
FW: And the cheapest... (dissolves in laughter)
PB: I just want to say that while this was going on... what were we doing, Fran?
FW: We were trying to / FW & PB: save the film... / FW: from the
    …. clutches of the pirate.

Ladies, I am very sorry you failed.

18. HARRY POTTER AND THE WRITING OF FICTION

I enjoyed Ms. Rowling's popular series, a series that is of interest to me both as a reader and as a writer of fantasy/adventure novels.

Imagination, characterization, coherence, and grammar are important in fiction. Let us look at the novels from these four viewpoints.

Imagination: Ms. Rowling deserves high praise for creating a fascinating and complete world. As a "worldsmith" she ranks with Tolkien—and, unlike JRRT, she was able to complete her vision during her lifetime. Arguments I have seen that disdain her achievement on grounds that "school novels" are not new are invalid because the whole measure of an author's imagination is how well the author renovates and refreshes old themes. The idea of a dual world, of a school for magicians, of the many elements of that world and that school, are all praiseworthy achievements well worked out in the books. Ms. Rowling deserves very high marks for imagination.

Characterization: Ms. Rowling has created characters we like to read about. What can be more important in a work of fiction? She populates her universe with a vast and well-drawn citizenry. The three main characters are very likeable; we enjoy watching them grow. The Hogwarts faculty is an interesting group. We "love to hate" the Dursleys and the other villains. Severus Snape is a very fine creation, both infuriating in his obsessive unfairness to Harry and puzzling in his ambiguity. The author takes time to develop many secondary characters; Horace Slughorn, for example, the would-be power behind thrones who hopes, from his comfortable apartments, to influence the greater world by cultivating those students whom he believes will rise to positions of wealth and power, is intriguing and amusing—a relative, perhaps, of Professor Sillery in Anthony Powell's *Dance to the Music of Time*. High marks, again, for Ms. Rowling's galaxy of fine characters!

Coherence: By this word I mean internal cohesion, plot logicality, believability within the created world.

Ms. Rowling develops her story over seven volumes in a well-planned plot arc. The growth of Voldemort from a menacing rumor through threatening reality is handled well.

However, I feel that Ms. Rowling often fails in inducing the reader to accept events as reasonable or logical and often stretches suspension of disbelief beyond any reasonable elasticity..

The chief reason for this failure is her magic system. All fantasy authors must deal with magic: where does it come from, how is it used, who can use it, what can it do, what price is paid for its use? Ms. Rowling takes the easiest way out. Those who possess magic can, even at the age of eleven or twelve, use much of it with a minimum of training, in unlimited quantities, with no price at all attached. Magic can defy gravity, charm and curse, jinx and hex, heal and harm, and even create things from nothing (a power traditionally limited to an almighty God)— all this with the flick of the wrist and a couple of words of fake Latin. It does not even tire the magician.

One problem with this system is that the reader must ask, many times (and I will spare you examples; you can think of them yourself), "Why doesn't he wave his wand and solve the problem by...?"

The wand is also the equivalent of a pistol in the Old West: victory comes to the quickest on the draw (except that it is a lot harder for a gunman to hit anything with a pistol than it is for a child magician to levitate or petrify an opponent). I wonder why special holsters for wands are not part of the wizarding world.

Sudden and artificial solutions to plot problems abound. The most flagrant example is perhaps the Room of Requirement; one might say that this room helps the author more than it helps Harry or Draco. When the author needs a place for events that could not possibly happen in any well-regulated school, the Room appears at her call. House Elves also materialize as needed. And so on.

*

The notion that the wizarding world would be unknown to Muggles is itself incredible. With the bulk of wizards and witches coming from

53

mixed-blood or no-blood families, how could this world not have become common knowledge?

Grammar: No one could call Ms. Rowling's prose anything more than serviceable. She ignores some of the basic rules of writing fiction.

Her continual use of adverbs after direct quotes at first annoys and eventually infuriates anyone who is aware of how bad a trait this is. (My favorite is in *H-BP*, p. 336: "Oh, that one had a great vogue during my time at Hogwarts," said Lupin reminiscently.") Stephen King remarked, in a largely favorable review, that Ms. Rowling never met an adverb she disliked.

She tends to tell, not show—or to do both, as though the reader is too ignorant to figure out the significance of what is happening.

She repeats phrases too often, e.g. how many times are we told that Crookshanks has a "bottlebrush tail"?

Editors exist to correct such things. Why Ms. Rowling's publishers did not heavily edit her works is beyond me. (Possibly, with the later volumes, they did not care, as the books would sell well anyway; but surely in Volume One, when she was unknown? As soon as "Shoo!" said Mr. Dursley loudly" appeared on page 5, as soon as, on page 7, characters mumble and snap instead of say, the editor's red pen should have been busy. It would have helped immensely with the next six volumes for her to learn these things right away. Now she may never learn them at all.

Ms. Rowling's two booklets, *Magical Beasts and Where To Find Them* and *Quidditch Through the Ages*, are much better written than the novels. She does not have to struggle with dialogue and can always tell rather than show. Could her real talents as a writer of prose lie chiefly in the area of non-fiction?

Summing Up. For lovers of fantasy fiction, the strengths of the Harry Potter novels outweigh the weaknesses. But those who love great children's literature—and Harry Potter is, after all, intended primarily for the young—cannot, I think, be sure that this series will in the long run take a place with *The Wind In the Willows, Charlotte's Web, Pippi Longstocking* or *Winnie the Pooh*, to name a few immortal works.

19. THE DOME
(A Poem)

Oh muse! To Troy I need not roam
A noble epic theme to find:
I need not wander far from home
For inspiration; no, my mind
Of thoughts is full--in fact, inflated--
And my spirits are elated
And my ravished eyes dilated
As I contemplate THE DOME.

Vast expanse of supple plastic--
Strong and sleek and so elastic--
To our eyes a sight fantastic
Towering o'er the new-dug loam.
In its splendor so stupendous
In its grandeur so tremendous
Kind indeed the gods to send us
Such a marvel. Hail, O DOME!

To limn its glories sure requires
David's and Apollo's lyres,
Tolstoy's pen and heavenly choirs
And a very weighty tome.
Rapt with wonder we behold thee
As the air-pumps do unfold thee
And thy wonders yet untold be
Laid before us, mighty DOME.

Through all lands thy fame is ringing;
Guns are booming, choirs singing,
Cars are speeding, planes are winging,
Ships are tossing on the foam:
Kings and scholars, folk discerning,
All to Minnesota turning,
All consumed with febrile yearning
In their haste to view THE DOME.

Athens now will be forgotten,
London seem quite misbegotten,
And who gives a hoot for Rome?
Taj Mahal and Notre Dame, too.
Chartres? Invalides? Versailles? Pooh!
SSMS* has THE DOME.

----

* Shattuck-St. Mary's School

20. THE NEWEST MEMBERS OF THE UNITED NATIONS

GROSS KLEINREICH

Nestled between the Strumnitz and Flessgau Rivers, Gross Kleinreich, which seceded from Burgundy in 1422, is ruled by His Serene Highness Grand Duke Ottokar XXVII. The happy populace—by law, depressed and sulky people are hanged—lives in the only remaining Divine Right Absolute Monarchy in Europe. The duchy's primary products are overpriced sweatshirts sold to tourists and elaborate postage stamps bought only by philatelists. (Gross Kleinreich welcomes visitors, but, since it is not very large, please park in Luxembourg.)

TOUGOUBOUGOU

The Peoples' Democratic Republic of Tougoubougou was established in 1966 as a union of the Tougous and the Oubougous, two tribes on the lower Upper Volta River. Government is by coup d'état, and preserves the old Oubougou tradition that the new president cook and eat his predecessor. The national income is based on loans from the United Nations deposited directly into the president's Swiss bank account.

CARAMBA

Formerly a strip mall in Tijuana, the Republic of Caramba declared independence from Mexico in 1998, a move that succeeded because nobody noticed. The chief industry is digging tunnels to the U.S.A. and charging 50,000 pesos apiece to people who use them. The population —Señor Martinez, his wife, and their thirteen children—hopes to move to Los Angeles soon.

GUANONIA

The Grand Republic of Guanonia consists of two archipelagos in the South Pacific, the Teeniweeni Isles and the Itsibitsi Group. The population is approximately 3,000,000, ninety-eight percent of whom are birds that provide the islanders' cash "crop" and main export, from which the nation takes its name. This proud land—known in colonial times as the Gulldung Islands—is trying desperately to get some Western country to take it back.

21. TEMPERATURE LAG

We all know about jet lag, the effect caused by sudden transition between time zones and the subsequent necessity of adjusting one's "internal clock" to the new environment.

I wonder if a similar problem may be caused by extreme temperature changes. Minnesota usually has terrible winters. What is it like for visitors flying in from, say, Hawaii or Egypt to arrive in the arctic air of Minneapolis? Surely their internal thermometers need adjustment at least as much as their internal clocks.

How to solve this problem? Airplanes whose final destinations are much more frigid than their departure points could slowly reduce cabin temperatures en route. Beginning at a balmy 80° in Honolulu, passengers could be cooled into the sixties by the time they reach Los Angeles, the fifties by Salt Lake City, and so on until they reach the Twin Cities able to see their breath, at least somewhat prepared for the arctic conditions they face in the awful place they have, for whatever reasons, chosen to come to.

Airlines could also perform the reverse operation. People leaving the Land of 10,000 Lakes on a lovely June day could undergo increasingly miserable heat and humidity until, wilting, drenched in sweat, they get off at some inferno like New Delhi or Bangkok.

Airlines might thus increase business: some travelers, once they come to realize what a wretched place they are going to, could well decide to return as soon as they arrive, even at the expense of a pricey one-way ticket.

On the other hand, some folks might just abandon travel altogether. After all, there's no place like home.

22. A REVENGE ARIA A LA VERDI

Here is a bit of whimsy inspired by listening to Count Stankar's recitative and aria ("Disonorato io son!" and "Oh gioia inesprimibile") in Act III of *Stiffelio*.

Argument: In Acts I & II, Count Ammazarlo, learning that Baron Scellerato said hello to Innocenza, the count's daughter, without first having been properly introduced, considers all aspects of the outrage for almost a full minute before concluding that there is only one way (other than immediate suicide) to deal with such an insult. Accordingly, he accosts the baron at a party, where, after hinting at his disapproval of the baron's conduct by boxing his ears, spitting on his shoes, and pouring punch all over his doublet, he challenges him to a duel. The duel is duly fought (offstage), after which the Count appears on stage and sings:

Justice! Justice! I have found it! Halleluia! Praise the Lord!
Surely 'twas the hand of Heaven that directed my sharp sword:
As we parried, thrust, recovered, as we fought with might and main
I soon chopped him into fragments that now decorate the plain.

So the remnants of this person have been scattered far and wide
Once my blade went in his liver and came out the other side.
So the honor of my family is restored to pristine state
Now that Baron Scellerato can be henceforth called "the late."

My sweet daughter, Innocenza, I've protected all her life
For I've never met a man who could deserve to call her "wife."
And a father has a duty to keep libertines in line.
(She is only forty-seven and I'm only sixty-nine.)

In some countries family problems might be taken up in courts
With the lawyers and the judges scribbling stuff 'bout pleas and torts—
But down here in fair Italia we despise mere feeble prose
And defend all slights to honor by just carving up our foes.

Count Ammazarlo then hastens to church to ask pardon for any recent peccadilloes.

23. THE ADVENTURE OF THE SURPRISING ENDING

On a bright, sunny morning in central London—very odd weather that many found disconcerting —the greatest detective in the world sat behind his large desk sipping his customary cup of *tisane* while perusing the *Times.*

He closed the paper, thinking that today's lead article offered hope for the future: now that Mr. Chamberlain had become Prime Minister, surely England would at last begin to take a firm line against Herr Hitler and Signor Mussolini. It was high time: the clock on the wall said 10:13:27 AM, Friday, May 28, 1937 A.D. (The detective, impatient with slipshod clocks that provide only partial information, had had this one custom made in Zurich.)

The door to the outer office opened as there entered a tall, lean, handsome gentleman of perhaps fifty, attired in a neat grey suit and a regimental tie. This man radiated all that was fine in the British upper-middle class: honesty, plain dealing, bravery, trustworthiness, dependability.

"Cheerio, old bean! I say, what a simply spiffing morning, what?" he called out as he tripped on his own feet and went sprawling on his face. Fortunately the inch-thick pile of the fine mauve carpet prevented any injury.

The great detective contemplated this through his pince-nez and said, *"Eh bien, mon pauvre* Captain Waterloo, *vous êtes bien maladroit comme usuel, n'est-ce pas*? Please, arise and adjust your garments. Your cravat she has been much disorganized."

The former officer was spared further contumely by the rapid entry of a lady in early middle age, her dark blonde hair tied in a severe bun, her not unattractive figure mostly concealed by her modest blue dress. She proffered a handful of mail. "The first delivery, Mr. Greycelles," she said. "And there was a very urgent call from Viscount DeLuxe. He seemed to think he could speak to you at once, but I explained that you never accepted calls before 10:18½, after you finished your *tisane*. I told him you would return his call."

"Quite right, my dear Miss Kumquat," said her employer. "One must have order and method in one's life or it becomes like the existence of the wild beasts of the field. Did his Lordship hint at whatever *petit* problem troubles him?"

"He said that an explosion has destroyed the entire staff wing of Garrish Manor, his ancestral home, killing six retainers, including Mat Grubb, his Chief Gardener for forty years."

"Ah, these trifles," said Greycelles. "Call his Lordship and ask if his senior under-gardener survived. If, as I suspect, he was not even there— *probablement* he said he had to make a sudden visit to a sick great-aunt or other superannuated relative—then voilà! Gardeners know all about fertilizer, a prominent component of which, the nitrate of aluminum, is most useful in the making of *objets explosif* such as the bombs of time. As for motive, the man surely wished to supplant his senior, whose long tenure of office must have annoyed him."

As the efficient secretary hurried to make the call, Captain Waterloo, now seated on a sofa, exclaimed, "By Jove, Greycelles, aren't you jumping to conclusions? I mean…"

The soigné detective raised a plump hand. "*Doucement, mon vieux.* Énée Greycelles, he leaps not to the conclusions rash. Did I not just read in the *Times* that a hundred pounds of fertilizer was stolen last week from a warehouse in Little Rotting, a village not far from Garrish Manor? *Eh bien*, the under-gardener took it for the construction of the *bombe gigantesque* used in the up-blowing of his so-hated rival the chief gardener. So now we have solved two cases. Remind Miss Kumquat to bill both Viscount DeLuxe and the Little Rotting constabulary. But now let us peruse the mail and discover if any real problems await us, *mon ami.*"

The mail apparently contained only routine items: a bill from the Bulldog Breed Cleaners for £150 (the detective always had a suit cleaned after wearing it once), confirmation that four pallets of the finest *tisane* were en route from Brussels, advertisements from eight clothing stores and three manufacturers of moustache wax. But upon reaching the last item Greycelles exclaimed, "*Tiens! Voyez*, Waterloo, a coronet on this so-expensive envelope." Quickly he ran his Damascus-steel letter opener under the edge and withdrew a magnificent sheet of paper. "*Mon cher ami*, we are bidden to see the Duke of Worcestershire at Daggerthrust House, his summer residence in Kent. His Grace recalls fondly how I found his missing cuff link two years ago and now has another matter about which he wishes to consult us."

"A bit of all right, that," said the captain. "I can run us down in my new Bugatti 57T. I've installed patent feeder gaskets on the supercharger and chromed the reverse valve injectors so the gidgit pump maximizes the superflow. Goes like smoke, old chap."

The detective peered over his pince-nez. "I have no idea what you just said, but from your animation I infer that you can provide adequate transport to St. Anspeth-on-Sea-by-Marsh, the village where Daggerthrust House has its location. Excellent. We leave in three days. I shall have just time enough to groom my moustache."

Before Greycelles and Waterloo left for lunch, Miss Kumquat reported that Viscount DeLuxe's senior sub-gardener had been arrested and had confessed to both the bombing and the theft of the fertilizer. "His Lordship sends his undying thanks for your miraculous insight," she said. "And the Little Rotting police are eternally grateful, especially since they had grown very tired of interrogating every tramp they could find."

"*Mais naturellment*," replied her chief. "But fail not to send the bills promptly."

(2)

"I say! What a pile!" exclaimed Captain Waterloo as his sleek Bugatti passed under the portcullis of Daggerthrust House.

Énée Greycelles had spent most of the trip with his hat pulled over his eyes while he fingered his rosary: at times the car had been moving at fifty miles per hour. Now he relaxed and adjusted his suit. "*Enfin*, we arrive," he said. "I congratulate you on your good luck, Waterloo, in not killing us both. *Oui*, this *maison magnifique* is impressive, *n'est-ce pas*? She was built in the fifteenth century and often attacked and defended. But inside these ancient walls are found the most modern conveniences, including the central heating of the bedrooms, thank heaven. Even in June one may experience the chills nocturnal."

As liveried lackeys hastened to unload Captain Waterloo's portmanteau and Énée Greycelles's three trunks, the captain asked his friend about the Duke of Worcestershire.

"Marmaduke Phyffe-Drumme is an aristocrat most eminent," replied Greycelles. "His title, of course, derives from the piquant condiment his ancestors concocted and whose secret recipe they sold to Messrs. Lea and Perrins in return for a share of the subsequent enormous profits. The current Duke fought most valiantly in the late war, or rather would have, had he not fallen off the gangway upon his arrival in France and so disrupted his leg that he was invalided from the army and sent home to serve in the garrison of Edinburgh for four years. Even today he walks with the limp. He inherited the title when his father was killed at the Somme. His Grace has experienced other sorrows. His twin brother—his junior by three minutes—died of an *attaque cardiaque*, and his wife the Duchess also suffered a disappointment."

"What was that?"

"She died. A fall off her horse. The marriage had not been blessed with children."

"Then who is his heir?"

"The Duke had a younger brother, Dudley, who died at Passchendaele. This man's son, Bertie, is the heir. He is, alas, the—how do you say?—the *mouton noir* of the family, the sheep who is black. Although enrolled at the famous Cambridge, he studies not hard and runs about with flappers and other *décadents*. The Duke hopes the young man is but knitting his wild oats…"

"Sowing, you mean."

"*Merci.*"

Crustley, the head butler, came out to escort the two men to his Grace, who received them in his study. "Greycelles, so good to see you," he exclaimed, rising and advancing with a noticeable stiffness of his right leg to shake hands.

"Your Grace, may I present *mon ami* and associate Captain Waterloo."

"Welcome to Daggerthrust House, captain. What was your regiment?"

"The 77th, sir."

"Ah yes, the Sussex, Sherwood, and Shropshire Sharpshooters. Fine outfit. Please, sit down."

The Duke rang a bell. A maid entered with a tray of drinks, curtsied, and withdrew.

The Duke looked gravely at his guests. "Greycelles, I'm up a tree. I hope you can help."

"If your Grace will describe his problem, I am hopeful to help him descend from the *arbre*."

"My watch has disappeared. Vanished. I removed it before taking a bath two days ago. When I returned to my dressing room the bally thing was gone. Nothing else missing: note-case, pen, monocle, all still on the dresser. But not my watch."

"Had this timepiece any extraordinary value?" asked the detective.

"Well, it is an heirloom. Belonged to my great-grandfather, and always passed to the eldest son. Very nice gold case with the family crest engraved inside. But not very valuable as such, I should think."

"And easily identified," said Greycelles. "Waterloo, tell Miss Kumquat to telephone the pawnshops to assure that it has not been so disposed of. But so conspicuous an object would not be likely to end up there. Your servants, your Grace—could one of them have abstracted it?"

"Never. Only Crustley and the evening maid, Tilly, were in the main house. He is absolutely trustworthy—my batman in the war, you know, a former Lance-Bombardier—while she was listening to the radio in the scullery. Crustley saw her. Anyway, if it were a domestic, surely my money would also have been taken? Damn sight more negotiable than the watch."

"*Bien sûr*, your Grace. You have reason. May I ask what people of quality were in the house?"

"There were six—still are, in fact. My friend Sir Augustus Wall-Nutt, 7th Baronet Nutt of Nutt House, his wife Lady Honoria, and their daughter Arabella; my nephew Bertie; my secretary Belle Sans-Merci; and an American furniture expert, Clem Visigoth, who represents a firm in New York interested in buying some of my antiques. You'll meet them all at supper."

"*Trés bien.* I shall submit them all to psychological study."

"But surely you don't suspect any of *them* of stealing my watch?" asked the Duke, tugging nervously at his moustache.

The great detective shrugged. "The objects physical, they do not vanish into the thin air, your Grace. If the watch is gone, someone took it. If, as you say, the servants could not have done so, it may have been a guest. Do the others know of your loss?"

"Oh yes, I've mentioned it more than once."

"Then I will see you at dinner, your Grace. As that is only a few hours away, I must now start on my *toilette* so as to be presentable."

(3)

Greycelles met briefly with his associate before going down to the Great Hall. "Waterloo, you must ascertain whether there any animals in the house. It is possible that some furry creature, attracted by the gleam of the ducal timepiece, abducted it. Also determine if in this region are many crows or other large birds and if there are windows in the room. We must be certain that a flying beast did not make off with the watch, in the way of *la gazza ladra* in the Rossini opera of the same name, where a magpie is the real thief of the missing items."

"Rightyoh," replied the captain as he accidentally knocked a shaving cup onto the floor. "I'll stir my stumps and get cracking."

(4)

Dinner, with nine covers, was served at 7:00. At the head of the table sat his Grace, his jacket adorned with several decorations from the King that he had earned by being born. On his right was his nephew Bertie, whose youthful good looks were marred by drooping eyelids and puffy cheeks. To his left, Lady Honoria, still lovely, in an attractive emerald gown, with her husband, Sir Augustus, beside her. Their daughter Arabella sat on the opposite end of that side of the great table, beside Bertie—a serious-looking young woman in plain black.

Belle Sans-Merci sat on one end, next to Sir Augustus; her rather low-cut dress and carefully-painted countenance suggested a concern with external appearance greater than that normally associated with a secretary. At the other end of the table was the American antiquities authority, a man scarcely thirty who, bright-eyed and eager, appeared in coat and tie because he possessed no evening dress.

The arrival of Énée Greycelles and Captain Waterloo occasioned some uncertainty among the other guests. The Duke rose and said, "We are pleased to have with us today a man who will need no introduction, for he is illustrious. May I present someone whom I can confidently describe as the world's greatest detective, a master sleuth of such renown that I need hardly say his name…"

As these encomia fell on his feasted ears, Énée Greycelles's lips formed a characteristic little smirk of self-satisfaction below his impeccable moustache. But all at once the Duke's fine words were interrupted as Clem Visigoth, who had been listening with growing excitement, sprang up and exclaimed, "I've heard of you. Gosh all geewhillikers, this is neat! I never thought when I came to England I'd get to meet Sherlock Holmes!"

The glacial silence that fell as the other guests exchanged glances was finally broken by a sigh from Lady Honoria that sounded a bit like "Oh God."

"This is Énée Greycelles," said the Duke firmly. "And his colleague Captain Waterloo."

Mr. Visigoth did a double take, then grinned and said, "Well I'm hornswoggled. That's one on me. Anyone have a towel so's I can wipe the egg off my face? But *your* name's familiar, captain. Why, I arrived in London at the train station your family's named after."

Only the collective exercise of several stiff upper lips prevented pandemonium after this new gaffe. Waterloo smiled a little painfully and said, "Actually, old bean, it's not the station. Waterloo is a town…"

"In Iowa, sure," said Visigoth. "But I didn't hardly reckon your people would be from the Midwest. Ever been to Cedar Rapids? That's just down the road a piece."

This mystifying question went unanswered when the Duke said, forcefully, "Mr. Greycelles has agreed to help find my missing watch."

"Oh, uncle, is that really necessary?" Bertie Phyffe-Drumme looked languidly up from his contemplation of the tablecloth. "I mean isn't that rather like calling in the Duke of Wellington to put down a small riot?"

"Ah no, monsieur," said the detective. "The crimes so small, they are often most interesting."

"Crime?" Sir Augustus looked and sounded most surprised. "Has there been one? His Grace just misplaced his watch, surely."

The Duke affixed his monocle in his right eye, gazed around the table, and said, "I did not misplace it. As I have said more than once, it vanished whilst I was bathing—and nothing else did, which is damned mysterious."

"*Exactement,*" said Greycelles. "*Pourquoi* did the note-case remain? And the pen most valuable? No, *mes amis*, this theft is *trés mysterieux*. Later this evening I shall wish to speak with each of you. But let us now enjoy this fine repast."

The detective's words put something of a damper on conviviality, implying as they did that all the guests were suspected of theft. Conversation was minimal for several minutes as liveried flunkies brought each course. Then young Arabella Wall-Nutt asked Mr. Visigoth what he thought of Benito Mussolini and Lady Honoria spoke to the Duke in praise of his gardens and asked particularly how he managed to grow such marvelous snapdragons. Sir Augustus asked Greycelles what he thought of the meal. When the detective, who had been sampling each dish with the acumen of a gastronome, replied, "*C'est excellent. His Grace must have a *maître-chef* most *formidable*," the baronet said, "Indeed he does—Anatole. Without peer, that man. And a countryman of yours, I imagine."

"No, Sir Augustus, I am not French."

"Ah, of course. Belgian, correct?"

"Mais non. I am a Luxembourger, from Troisvierges, in the Francophone district of the Grand Duchy—a district of only about a thousand acres, but from there I come."

Captain Waterloo, a hearty trencherman, carried on a desultory conversation with Mlle. Sans-Merci, whom, he noticed, kept trying to attract the eye of Bertie Phyffe-Drumme; but that young man seemed indifferent to her, eating slowly, apparently preoccupied with deep thoughts.

(5)

After the ice cream and wafers, Énée Greycelles carefully wiped his mouth, smoothed his moustache, and went to a small drawing room, to which the guests were summoned one by one. Captain Waterloo sat quietly

66

nearby, striving, as he always did, to learn the art of detection from his friend. But the interviews did not seem to him to be very productive. The watch had disappeared between 5:00 and 6:30 PM on May 26. During this time Sir Augustus had been visiting the ducal kitchens and wine cellar with Anatole, his wife had been promenading in the gardens with the head gardener, Mr. Visigoth had been scrutinizing the furniture in the Great Hall with Crustley as his guide, Miss Wall-Nutt had been in the library reading about the Italian conquest of Ethiopia, observed by Bertie and Belle playing badminton on the lawn outside the library windows.

"*Tiens*!" exclaimed Greycelles when he was done. "These guests all have the alibis, how do you say, dressed in metal."

"Ironclad," suggested Captain Waterloo.

"*Oui. Eh bien*, and your inspection of the dressing room and the animals domestic?"

"A wash-out, old chap. The windows were open but have screens, so no birds could have gotten in. There are no pets—the Duke is allergic to dander. Of course there is a pack of foxhounds, but their kennel is well away from the house, and fenced. I checked all the drawers and closets."

"*Tant pis*. Let us inspect further the house. Perhaps something will appear."

But nothing appeared. They met an elderly maid carrying a tray of food down a corridor and a footman polishing tables, but as they neared the library and the sound of the guests inside, Greycelles appeared no closer to a discovery. Then he exclaimed, "Waterloo, are these people playing charades?"

"Sounds it. Great fun don't you think?"

"For you English, perhaps. Charades, like the warm beer and the cricket, are part of your national character. But to a Luxembourger, non. *Nous avons une phobie de* charades. Please tell his Grace I must retire early and will see him in the morning." He hurried off as fast as he could waddle, leaving his friend to face an evening of The Game.

(6)

Breakfast at Daggerthrust House was an informal buffet—one went in at any time from 8 to 10. Énée Greycelles was finishing his oatmeal when Captain Waterloo arrived and sat down to porridge, eggs, sausage, bacon, tomato, toast and marmalade, and a pot of tea.

"Not very peckish, old chap?" asked Waterloo. "Or are you banting—trying to lose a bit?"

"I do not begin the day with a three-course meal," was the reply. "When you finish your dietary orgy, I would like you to observe closely the second-floor corridor. You can do so by sitting in the gun room. Earlier this morning I saw an elderly maid carrying a food tray, just as we both saw last night."

"But I don't understand…"

"Naturally. I followed this maid from a distance. When I turned the corner she had vanished. Poof, she was not there. Where did she go? And why is food being carried to an area where no one lives? Let me know if there is any other unusual traffic in this area. Eat lunch there."

"If you say so, Greycelles. What are your plans?"

"I shall quietly observe the guests and converse with them—a most interesting group. I sense that something strange is going on—possibly several things, all of them unconnected with the missing watch. We shall meet again at luncheon."

Captain Hastings was puzzled, but, that being his usual condition when dealing with his friend, he just finished his meal and betook himself to the gun room, dividing his time between watching the second floor and examining the racks and cases of rifles, shotguns, fowling pieces, rook guns, small mortars, bows, crossbows, halberds, maces, swords, spears, and antique armor that form part of any English gentleman's household goods.

(7)

At 2:00 the two friends convened in the detective's bedroom. After lighting one of his tiny Moldavian cigarettes, Greycelles asked Waterloo if he had seen anything.

"Yes, I did. At about noon an elderly woman carried a tray of food past the gun room and around the corner into the next corridor. I strolled there—didn't want to appear to be following, of course—and I couldn't find her. I fancy I heard a sound like the closing of a door, though—perhaps the sliding of a panel."

"Good work, mon ami. *Trés bien.* We shall investigate this corridor."

"And you, did you discover anything?"

"A most interesting morning. Did you know that Sir Augustus Wall-Nutt's cook is retiring in a month? The baronet is distressed—he likes to keep a fine table. And his wife, the Lady Honoria, is a gardener most passionate, a member of several floral societies and an entrant in many competitions. She especially favors the *gueule-de-loup,* what you call the snapdragon and we the wolf's throat. Miss Wall-Nutt is an unusual young woman. Far from being fascinated by the dances and the young men and her *maquillage,* the make-up, she is most seriously concerned with international politics and history. She is especially delighted by the policies of *Il Duce,* for whom she has the highest regard."

"Is that why she wears black dresses?"

"You laugh, but yes, I think she wears then in emulation of the black shirts. The young Bertie, he on the other hand probably does not know where Italy is, but can tell you the results of all the high-stakes races held in the last four years. I fear he is in financial difficulties most serious."

Greycelles took a sip of water before going on. "This Mlle. Sans-Merci, I believe she is not just the Duke's secretary, if you comprehend. But she may sense the sun is setting and seek a new attachment, with the heir. A most seductive lady."

"And the American?"

"Oh, *mon Dieu*, I spoke to him for half an hour. It was most difficult to comprehend many of the sounds he makes. I believe my English to be quite good, but what he speaks, is that English? But there is no doubt that he is most knowledgeable about *les meubles d'époque*—that is, antiques—and extremely desirous of acquiring valuable objects for the firm that employs him. But I have a suspicion I must investigate more thoroughly."

"So what is our next step?" asked Waterloo, rising and knocking over his chair.

"I must speak with Anatole, the chef, and the head gardener, and also lurk in the library. You keep an eye upon M. Bertie and Mlle. Sans-Merci. We will convene after supper."

(8)

The guests were on time for the evening meal but the Duke was not. This occasioned some surprise, for his Grace was a most punctual man.

The eight people nibbled dinner rolls and made small talk as they awaited the lord of the manor. Énée Greycelles was unusually animated, saying some words to everyone. He asked Sir Augustus if he was making progress in finding a new chef. "Indeed I am," replied the baronet. "I received encouraging news only today."

"Here in Kent?" asked the detective.

"By phone, of course, from the London agency I employ in the search."

"Oh yes, of course. And my lady Honoria, you enter I think another floral tournament?"

"This summer, monsieur. The great Snapdragon Concourse will be held in late August. I have every hope of triumphing over the Duchess of Devon. I have been determined to annihilate that woman for years. The day is soon coming when she will wilt and I will bloom, so to speak. I shall make the name of Wall-Nutt illustrious in the highly-competitive snapdragon field."

"I wish you *bonne chance*, my lady. And you, Miss Arabella—did you not tell me that you plan a trip to Rome in August?"

"Oh yes, and I so look forward to it, monsieur. My friends at the Italian Embassy say I may even have an audience with *Il Duce*! I hope I am worthy of meeting him."

"You have many friends among the Italian diplomats, mademoiselle?"

"Well, the assistant military attaché, *Tenente di Vascello* Julio Vermicelli, is helping me improve my Italian, so I often go there."

"And Mr. Visigoth, your work here goes well?"

"Sure enough. I pretty much finished the furniture and now I'm working on the smaller stuff—the Duke's got some pretty nice knickknacks kicking around the place."

"Such as the quattrocento pen holder in the study and the icon of St. Simeon Stylites in the chapel?"

"Well, I'll be jiggered! You sure know your antiques, Mr. Greycelles. Yeah, those two and the bronze miniature of George and the Dragon in the entryway are the best gewgaws in this whole dump."

"I imagine your firm did careful research on what you might find before sending you all the way from New York?"

"Natch. The Duke sent us Kodaks and descriptions of most of his stuff."

"Ah. You look *ravissant çe soir*, mademoiselle," he said to the ducal secretary as he lit her cigarette in its long holder. The lady smiled powerfully and replied, "*Merci beaucoup*, monsieur. One always tries to make a good impression." And her eyes strayed to Bertie Phyffe-Drumme, who, unlike the previous evening, was gazing at her with admiration.

"I am trying to make a good impression too," said the young man with a rueful smile. "Uncle Marmaduke sometimes has a little trouble understanding how expensive it is to live in the outside world when one is an orphan."

Further conversation was curtailed by Crustley opening the door and announcing "His Grace."

In came the Duke of Worcestershire, impeccably attired as usual, his right leg dragging a bit. He walked to the head of the table, took out his watch, consulted it, and said, "Sorry to be a bit after time. I was just tying up something. Please, let us begin."

Of course the reaction from all were exclamations and ejaculations that had the same general meaning: you found it!

Énée Greycelles noted a momentary hesitation before the Duke replied, "Oh, why yes, the watch. You know, I found it in the dresser. Can't think why I didn't remember putting it there. Sorry about that, Greycelles. You'll still receive a consulting fee for your efforts. Be off in the morning, I imagine?" He fixed his monocle in his left eye and gazed at the detective.

"*Bien sûr*, your Grace; if there is no more mystery, my presence here is superfluous, to be sure. But, with permission, I should like tonight to see more of your *château magnifique*."

Although it seemed that a slightly suspicious look clouded the ducal countenance, his Grace replied, "Of course, of course. Daggerthrust House is well worth seeing. Poke about as you like."

(9)

No sooner was supper ended than Greycelles and Waterloo withdrew. "*Vite, mon ami*, to the gunroom *immédiatement*," whispered the detective.

"You're really that eager to avoid charades?"

"Tcha! We must investigate the corridor while the others linger over their port, or whatever the English upper classes do after a meal. All my suspicions have been confirmed."

"Suspicions, Greycelles? I didn't know you had any."

"Did you not see? No, of course not. No matter. Ah, we arrive."

The detective began tapping the walls with his gold-handled cane as the two men walked slowly along. Soon came a hollow noise indicating the wall was not solid. "Inspect this area carefully," said Greycelles.

They did so, and Waterloo soon exclaimed, "What ho! A button behind this painting."

He pushed it and watched in amazement as a panel slid back. A moment later the two men stood in a narrow passageway that opened into a large room with doors on either side. The panel slid closed. Greycelles went to one door, the captain to the other, and it was Waterloo who called out, "Good lord! Greycelles, it's the duke. Or another duke."

A man was tied to a chair by ropes around his arms and legs, a gag in his mouth. Greycelles removed the gag. "I trust your Grace is not harmed?" he said.

"Greycelles! Waterloo! Thank heavens! I've been trussed up here for hours. Montague said he'd bring me supper but there's no telling what might actually happen."

"Have no fears, my lord. All will now be well."

"I don't want a scandal, you know. Monty isn't dangerous, really, except a bit when the moon is full. Can we get him back?"

71

"*Certainement*, when he arrives with the supper. But what of the aged servant?"

"Old Hepzibah knows about him. Monty surprised me when I visited him, tied me up, and told her I was having a fit. She hardly could be expected to suspect a substitution."

"*Trés bien*. We will make a resubstitution."

Captain Waterloo had listened to all this with increasing amazement on his honest face. Now he exclaimed, "Are you twins?"

"Yes, mon ami," replied Greycelles. "The person in the dining room is Montague Phyffe-Drumme, the younger twin brother of the Duke. His reported death was a ruse. He has been living in this not-uncomfortable apartment for some time, to avoid the necessity of placing him in a *maison de fous*, how do you say, a house of the mad. He somehow escaped, first stole the watch that represented to him the right of succession, returned here, and two days later, after tying up his brother, now impersonates him. Is not that so, your Grace?"

"Yes, yes it is. Poor old Mad Monty, as the family called him, was never quite right in the head. I decided to confine him here, in comfort, to avoid the public disgrace of putting a Phyffe-Drumme in the booby hatch after he announced that he was moving to Peru to be with his fellow llamas. His problem is periodic—usually he's nearly normal, then these fits come on him. I tried reasoning with him this time. Told him the greatest detective in the world was here for the watch and that his imposture was certain to be discovered. But he would not listen. I hope he doesn't go doolally tonight."

"We can but hope," replied Greycelles.

"But I say, how did you figure all this out?" asked Waterloo. "It seems like magic."

"Ah, I have as usual amazed you, *mon ami*?" asked Greycelles. "The bringing of food to this remote part of the manor naturally suggested a concealed apartment, as did the vanishing of the servant and the sound of a sliding door. In the library I read the newspaper account of the decease of Lord Montague and noted that he was interred at a very private funeral in the estate chapel. I concluded he might not have died at all. The appearance of the false duke with the watch clearly showed that something strange was afoot, for how could he have, as he said, just found it in a drawer? Did we not search the room thoroughly? But the decisive point was his wearing of the monocle in his left eye. Surely you noticed that the real Duke affixes it in his right one? Lord Montague remembered to imitate the limp, but not the monocle. *Enfin*, we search the corridor and *voilà*, the mystery she is solved."

"Brilliant," said Waterloo.

"Masterful," said the Duke.

"But of course," said Énée Greycelles with the archness he so often employed with those of slower intelligence—that condescending air of immeasurable intellectual superiority that endeared him to his intimates to such an extent that both Captain Waterloo and Miss Kumquat sometimes had to use all their strength to resist the urge to bludgeon his egg-shaped head with the nearest heavy object.

(10)

About an hour later Montague Phyffe-Drumme entered the hidden rooms carrying a bag of sandwiches. Confronted by three men with ropes and maces taken from the gunroom, he said, "Oh, dash it all, I see the jig is up," and submitted without a struggle.

"You know this is for your own good, Monty," said his brother. "I plan to bring in an alienist from Munich to treat you, and there's a chap in Zagreb whom I'm looking at as well. We may yet find a cure."

"Yes, yes, I know. But Marmaduke, I did so want to be Duke of Worcestershire even if it was only for a few hours. After all, I'm only two minutes younger than you. How nice it was down there, with everyone fawning on me and pretending they were interested when I told them all about llamas. They even said they wanted to hear about alpacas, and vicuñas too. And the charades were such fun. They always let me win."

His brother looked at him with a slightly tearful eye. "Have courage, Monty. We may get you back to normal yet. Now you go beddy-bye and have a nice nappy."

"All right, Marmaduke. I'll see you tomorrow. Oh, you had better take this." He smiled wanly as he handed his brother a large gold watch.

(11)

"I cannot thank you both enough," said the Duke as the three men walked to the dressing room so his Grace could freshen up after his ordeal. "But I fear, M. Greycelles, that I cannot very well announce your success to my guests. They must not know about Monty."

"*Je comprends tout*, milord" replied the detective. "I am discretion itself. The role of Captain Waterloo and myself shall remain secret. And since you—that is, your *pauvre frère*—asked me to leave in the morning, I shall do so."

"I knew you would understand," said the Duke. "I assure you my remuneration will compensate for your inability to reveal your masterful deductions."

12

The morning, however, brought travails that neither Greycelles nor Waterloo had expected. At breakfast and in the hour following, each of the guests managed to see the detective and his friend in order to sneer at them. Greycelles's insinuation on the first night that one of them had stolen the watch led to considerable raillery. "Are you sure you searched the dresser?", "You're not going to expect a fee for doing nothing, are you, monsieur?", "Losing your edge a bit, maybe?", "Well, we all go over the hill eventually," and "Rather blotted your copybook, eh, old boy?" were among the shafts aimed at him.

"*Parbleu!*" he finally exclaimed to Captain Waterloo. "These English snobs, they are insufferable. I lose the edge, eh? I am incompetent?"

"That American chap wasn't any nicer," said the captain. "At least I think that saying you 'fumbled the pass' and that you 'struck out' are not meant to be compliments."

"Very well, they seek to insult Greycelles, then Greycelles shall show them. Waterloo, ask the entire company to assemble in the library so I can bid them a fond *adieu*."

13

They did assemble, with the Duke. When all were seated expectantly, the detective stood and smiled sardonically. "*Mesdames et messieurs*, I must bid you farewell. But before I depart, I would like to say a few words. Although I was asked only to find the missing watch, I feel my duty to my client requires me to mention a few trivial matters I happened to notice in the course of my investigation."

He paused a moment, then began: "Sir Augustus, I am sorry to tell you that your efforts to hire his Grace's master chef away from him will not be successful. I pointed out to Anatole, after he revealed your secret efforts when I questioned him, that cooking for a great nobleman like the Duke of Worcestershire is far more prestigious than cooking for a mere baronet."

"And Lady Honoria, I fear I must reveal that your luggage contains several packets of snapdragon seeds that you took from the greenhouse and that two seedlings are concealed somewhere in your room. Your attempt to pass off the *magnifique* Ducal snapdragons as your own is going to fail."

"Miss Arabella, last night I observed you in the library placing in your reticule copies of the military plans for the defense of the county, which the Duke possesses in his capacity of Lord Lieutenant of Kent. No doubt you thought that presenting them to *Il Duce* when you visit Italy would please both the great dictator and your friends in the *chemises noires* at the Italian embassy."

"Master Bertie, his Grace may wish you to return the stack of fifty-pound notes you received from your accomplice after she removed them from the petty-cash drawer near the kitchen. The accomplice was of course you, Mademoiselle Sans-Merci, as part of your efforts to win over the ducal heir now that you are tired of his uncle."

"And Monsieur Visigoth, I congratulate the artisans at your firm in New York who provided you with forgeries of the so-precious pen holder, the icon, and the statuette that you have substituted for the real ones. The theft might not have been discovered until years after the originals were sold on the so-lucrative black market of art, *n'est-ce pas*? But thanks to the observations of Énée Greycelles your efforts are foiled and you are, how do you Yankees say, up a stream without a paddler, *hein*?"

The various exclamations, objurgations, maledictions, and outraged looks occasioned by the detective's remarks ceased at once when the Duke, who had been turning purple as the catalogue of crime continued, rose to his feet. His monocle popped from his eye. "By Jove!" he trumpeted. "I have been sheltering a whole nest of vipers in my bosom. I never heard of... I am going to fetch my favorite shotgun and a good supply of rock salt, and if any of you wretches are here when I return, I shall give you something you will long remember. Mr. Greycelles, Captain Waterloo, remain here. I want to express my gratitude."

Fortunately for the guests, the Duke's bad leg meant it would be some little time before he could get to the gunroom and back. The six thieves took Lady Macbeth's advice: they stood not upon the order of their going but went at once, leaving behind not only the various purloined items but most of their luggage. Gravel spurted from beneath the tires of Vauxhalls, Bentleys, and Rolls-Royces in the mad dash to get away; soon a cloud of dust hung over the portcullis of Daggerthrust House.

The detective and his friend watched this precipitate exodus with smiling satisfaction. "*Bien*," said Greycelles. "My copybook she is again clean, I am returned from across the hill."

"Rather!" exclaimed Waterloo. "I say, ripping good show, Greycelles. I had no idea you were so busy watching these people."

"Énée Greycelles, he sees all, *mon ami*. My close observation of this collection of buffoons easily produced the discoveries I have just related."

The Duke returned some minutes later carrying his trusty 20-gauge. "I suppose they all scarpered?" he asked with a grim smile. "Good for them. What a parcel of rogues. I am very grateful, Greycelles, very grateful indeed. But I must ask, had they not irritated you by their insults, were you planning to tell me of their misdeeds?"

"But of course, your Grace. However I would have done so privately, not in the sensational manner I used, so you could have dealt with them without alarm. Alas, they so enraged me that I could not resist a more public unmasking of their delinquencies."

"Don't blame you a bit," said the Duke. "And I hope this check for £3,000 will compensate for the rudeness you suffered under my roof."

"My chagrin is already vanishing," said the detective, smiling as he stowed the document in his note case.

Crustley entered to inquire if the Duke needed anything. "Return the shotgun and shells to the gun room," said his master. "And, as Miss Sans-Merci is no longer a member of the household, tell my agent in London to find me a new mistress. I mean secretary."

"At once, my lord," said the faithful retainer as he withdrew.

"Would you care to remain for a few days?" asked the Duke. "I should be delighted."

"*Merci beaucoup*, your Grace. But only this morning I received a call from Miss Kumquat to tell me of some incidents that have puzzled the police. Sir Usorius Greede, the banker, has been found dead in his study with the door locked and the windows bolted, but the authorities think it may not be suicide because the bullet holes were in his back and the gun was found in his left foot. Miss Vera Richley dropped dead at luncheon and there are some suspicions cast upon her nephew and heir since a servant heard him say nervously, as he passed her a cup, "Dear auntie, would you like some cyanide?" And then there is the matter of the American cotton magnate, Charlie Bollweevil, who came to London to negotiate a business deal and was last seen being escorted into an opium den by a Chinese, a Lascar, an Arab, and Major N.B.G. Pander, a most notorious man. My friend at Scotland Yard, Grand Inquisitor Sapp, as usual desires my assistance to investigate these little problems."

"I see you will be busy," said the Duke. "But please visit Daggerthrust House sometime soon. In a month or so I hope to have a more respectable circle of friends."

In an hour the car was loaded with luggage and a crate of Worcestershire sauce the Duke insisted on giving the detective. As Captain Waterloo started the engine of his sleek Bugatti, the Duke, waving goodbye, turned to Crustley and asked, "Have you seen my gold tie clip? I could have sworn I was wearing it this morning."

"*Vite, mon ami*," said Greycelles to Waterloo. "*Dépêchez-vous*, tread upon the accelerator."

The car sped away.

24. A CAUTIONARY TALE

Are you contemplating writing a novel? Do you long to see your name on the cover of a book published by some illustrious commercial enterprise? Have you succumbed to *furor scribendi*?

That's fine. You now have a worthwhile pastime to keep you busy. But before you start spending the advance you hope for, you might read this little article to learn (a) what might happen and (b) how long things can take.

Here is a chronology of the publishing history of *Storm Approaching*.

2001 – June 26 Began writing novel

2002 – July 29 Finished writing novel

2004 – June Finished editing and revising novel. (This could have taken less time, but I wrote the first drafts of the next two parts of the trilogy first)

2004 – Sept. Began agent search (103 query letters, 14.6% of which were successful, i.e. produced requests for a partial.)

2005 – April Secured fine agent. He suggested some changes; made changes, including about 20 pp. of new material.

2005 – by October Agent begins submissions to major publishers

Major publishers reject novel for various reasons; e.g. From Bantam: "This had an interesting premise and was indeed well written, but…" From Warner: "The plot is great and the pacing is good, but … the problem for me is the writing…" Very helpful.

2006 – March A "nibble" from a major publisher. First reader recommends book to Supreme Editor.

2006 – March through **2008** – August. Nothing happens. Agent repeatedly tries to get Supreme Editor to read book. Editor does not read book. Or maybe does. Or maybe reads part of it. Nobody knows.

<u>2008 – August</u> Agent gives up: Supreme Editor has maybe read book and did not like it and maybe will re-read it or maybe not. End of agented representation.

Author decides to self-publish novel as only alternative is burning it.

<u>2009 – May</u> *Storm Approaching* published at author's expense.

And now for the punch line:

<u>2012</u> – March Letter arrives from the Major Publisher. Excerpts below:

"Thank you… for your patience… We apologize sincerely for the delay, and are attempting to address our backlog and change our procedures… Please know that, because of the significant positive attributes of your manuscript, which the first reader enjoyed, it did reach the desk of an editor… Unfortunately, the editor did not find the manuscript right for [Major Publisher]…."

So there it is: a final answer after just six years. I am a bit surprised that all the principals—the author, the first reader, the Supreme Editor, even the agent—are still alive. As a historian I find it very comforting that, in this age of instant this and instant that, some things—in fact the whole of conventional publishing, as far as I can tell—still proceed at a pace that would have been considered stately when Charles Dickens—or Alexander Pope, for that matter—was trying to burst into print. When Augustus said *festina lente*, was he thinking of the publishing industry?

Patience is a virtue, and maybe sometimes a vice. If you hope to publish a book through a Major Publisher, start writing it today. You'll need all the time you've got.

Oh: Four volumes of the *Mercenary* series are now available, but not in bookstores. Why not buy the first volume today? Don't take your time…

25. A PENINSULAR BATTLE

Following his defeat at Sorauren in July 1813, Marshal Soult, pursued
by General Wellesley, began retreating to the French frontier.

Considerable amounts of French stores had been left at a village ten
miles southeast of Sorauren. Soult, not wishing to lose these valuable
supplies, detached an ad-hoc force to secure and evacuate them.

Wellesley, informed of this cache by Spanish guerrillas, sent a force of
British and Spanish troops to take the village and its contents.

Thus developed the ever-memorable Battle of Fuentes de Cucaracha (7
August 1813), where the British, Spanish, French, and some Germans
and Italians as well, fought perhaps the quintessential Napoleonic
battle.

1. COMMANDERS

The French force (11,000 men) was led by *Général de Division* Pierre
L'Heureux, whose experience in the wars had thus far been enjoyable,
if not indeed painless, for he had hardly been sober since the fall of the
Bastille. Born in 1767 at Ivry[1], Pierre had begun a career as the town drunk
(*l'ivrogne d'Ivry*) when, in 1787, his father, to get him out of town and
spare the family further disgrace, convinced a judge to sentence his son to
the army. Pierre tippled his way through the early stages of the revolution
as a private in the *Régiment de Picardie*. When many officers became
emigrés, he was made a *sous-lieutenant*, and by his placid acceptance of
Girondism, Jacobinism, the Terror, the Directory—whoever happened
to be in power—plus a talent for making bibulous but heartfelt patriotic
speeches to anyone who would listen, Pierre rose to a colonelcy by 1800.
Although he spent the Battle of Hohenlinden dozing in a wine vat behind
the town dump, his second covered for him—everyone rather liked the
amiable sot—so, in the general rejoicing after Moreau's great victory,
L'Heureux was promoted to *général de brigade*. He was then sent to
command the coast guards in the Department of Pyrénées-Orientales,
where he could do no harm. He married a vintner's daughter and became
a favored patron of every bar in Perpignan.

L'Heureux spent the glorious years 1801-1812 soaking up the culture
of his province and salting away a tidy sum in bribes from smugglers.
But in 1812, with the army greatly in need of officers for the Russian
Campaign, he received command of a brigade in Ney's corps; his slow
progress eastward to the seat of war was marked by empty champagne,
chianti, and schnapps bottles.

L'Heureux never could recall exactly what happened during the next
few months, but at Borodino he won the Legion of Honor: during the
assault on the flèches he became even more disoriented than usual and,
unaware of the retreat of Ledru's division, charged headlong into the
Russian lines, inspiring a renewed and successful French assault (in
which he was rescued, although wounded in the arm).

L'Heureux enjoyed his stay in Moscow: he personally looted the tsar's
wine cellar. He did not mind the great retreat, being far too pickled to feel
the cold (though it almost broke his heart when, outside Smolensk, he
had to abandon three wagonloads of vodka). On arrival in Germany he
was promoted—the Emperor praised his "fortitude and imperturbability
in the face of disaster"—and sent to Spain, arriving before Marshal Soult
learned that his new subordinate might not be the best man to entrust
with an independent command.

*Also marching towards the soon-to-be-stricken field was Major General Sir Marmaduke Doiley, K.C.B., with 19,000 men: eleven British regiments (nine infantry, two cavalry) and many Spaniards. Doiley, only 38, had had a serene career of promotions and favors by virtue of his greatest accomplishment: he was born rich. Although flunking out of two public schools and doing so poorly at Oxford that he had been awarded, uniquely, a *fifth*-class degree, Doiley's talent for making aristocratic friends and liberal doses of his father's money had put him in Parliament at the age of 23. There he did nothing at all. (This did not disappoint his constituents. Being elected by a rotten borough, he represented two orchards and a cemetery.) He did worm his way into the dissolute Carlton House set, assuring himself a busy career of wild parties, mistresses, and general debauchery. The Prince of Wales had him knighted in 1806 (in return for a large loan, which was never repaid). Deciding in 1808 to dabble at war, Doiley purchased a colonelcy and watched indulgently from Westminster as its lieutenant-colonel led it to die of cholera at Walcheren in 1809. Doiley than had his friends make him a major general. He commanded various units about the court; in 1812, sensing easy fame as the war in Spain drew to a close, he arranged to be sent there.

The future Duke of Wellington greeted Sir Marmaduke's arrival with a certain lack of enthusiasm ("His presence on the field is worth 40,000 men—to the French"). But Wellesley, not wishing to offend Doiley's high-placed friends, gave him several easy missions and an excellent chief-of-staff, Lt. Col. Harry Potts (who had fought in twenty battles but was socially disbarred from higher rank because his father was a shopkeeper).

Unfortunately, Col. Potts fell ill on 4 August, and Sir Marmaduke was on his own.

2. MOVEMENT TO CONTACT; THE BATTLEFIELD

The French would have arrived ahead of the British had not their tipsy commander taken a wrong turn that led them nine miles out of their way. The Anglo-Spanish army arrived on 6 August, a day ahead of the French. Gen. Doiley ordered the enemy supplies loaded on wagons for transport to Tolosa, hoping that neither his own troops nor his Spanish allies would loot them.

Gen. Doiley's hope that this mission would prove as easy as the others Wellesley had given him was spoiled that evening when Spanish cavalry scouts reported "thousands and thousands" of French troops approaching.

The sudden revelation that he would have to fight a pitched battle deeply stirred Gen. Doiley, but with true English aplomb he gave his subordinates no hint of his inner agitation (other than bursting into tears). The M.O. administered a mild sedative, its effects lasting until the French force began moving into sight and Doiley discovered that, in fact, it numbered considerably fewer men than did his own. At once recovering his sang-froid, the general began cudgeling his puny brains to concoct a plan for the next morning.

No such uncertainty was evident on "the other side of the hill." When Gen. L'Heureux's second, Gen. Fromage, reported that enemy troops held the town and were taking up positions north of it, the French commander gave a Gallic shrug and, momentarily taking his bottle of tequila from his lips, mumbled "Eh bien, zo attack zem." Realizing that this was probably as much command guidance as he would receive from his chief, at least in his present state, Fromage began disposing the corps.

*

The town of Fuentes de Cucaracha, a wretched collection of shacks and huts of surpassing squalor, was bisected by the River Burrito (also known as the "sewer of Navarre"), a sluggish but treacherous rivulet averaging twenty feet in width, too dangerous to cross except at bridges and fords. A small, noisome cork forest began southeast of the town and flourished, or at least grew, on either bank of the Burrito as far as the bridge. [See Map I] North of the town was a flat, grassy plain broken by small gullies and isolated trees. There were only two structures of note outside the town: the Royal Beehives and a stout stone farm. This farm was famous locally, built on a baptistery sacred to St. Hugo of Valencia known as Hugo's Font (often spelled as one word). Further north was a larger farm where bulls were raised for the ring. About two miles west was a line of hills, the Montañes de Tacos.

Doiley's plan was based on his belief (consistent with British strategy in the Napoleonic wars) that the chief duty of allies was to do the real work. He therefore decided to let his Spanish forces carry the weight of the assault. The Spaniards would be massed on the left to roll up the French right from Hugosfont to the road. The forest would be held by the marksmen of the 19th Rifles. The bulk of the other British troops would hold the line between the farm and the forest. One regiment, with

Damsey's R.H.A. battery, would cross the Burrito, circle south of the forest, and re-cross the river to strike the enemy left.

Having put together this scheme with the aid of his senior colonel (Trimble of the 28th), Doiley summoned his officers, issued his orders, and went to bed.

On the French side, Gen. Fromage planned an enveloping attack by his right to push the enemy into the Burrito. Having faced Spanish troops before, he did not fear them. Two-thirds of the corps (Divisions Fromage and Crapaud) was disposed on either side of Hugosfont, the 34th Light being detailed to take the place.

Fromage presented his plan to Gen. L'Heureux that night, as the Gallic commander was finishing his usual nightcap of vodka and absinthe. L'Heureux inspected the plans and threw up on them, which Fromage interpreted as approval.

3. THE SPANISH FURY (0700 – 0900)

As dawn broke the two camps stirred to life. Gen. Doiley rode north to the center of his line, where he found that the 44th Regiment (Archbishop of Canterbury's Own) had brewed a huge kettle of tea, from which he had a draught of "the cup that cheers but does not inebriate." About 1,500 yards eastwards, Gen. L'Heureux enjoyed a cup that did both, his usual "eye-opener," a pint of rum.

Both armies were drawn up by 0700. L'Heureux now perceived that the enemy forces seemed far more numerous than his own, but he was so used to seeing double that he mentally halved their numbers and ordered the advance to start. The divisions of Gens. Fromage and Crapaud marched off; the artillery of both sides opened fire.

Doiley sent a courier to the Spanish with orders to advance.

The Spanish forces were 10,000 infantry (the Division "Gloria o Muerte," whose battle flag bore a skull surmounting two bloody daggers) and 3,000 cavalry (the Dragoons of Enchilada, veterans of the first few minutes of many a fight). The Spanish were commanded by a wealthy grandee, the Duque de Plaza-Toro, who had earned his high position by being a wealthy grandee.

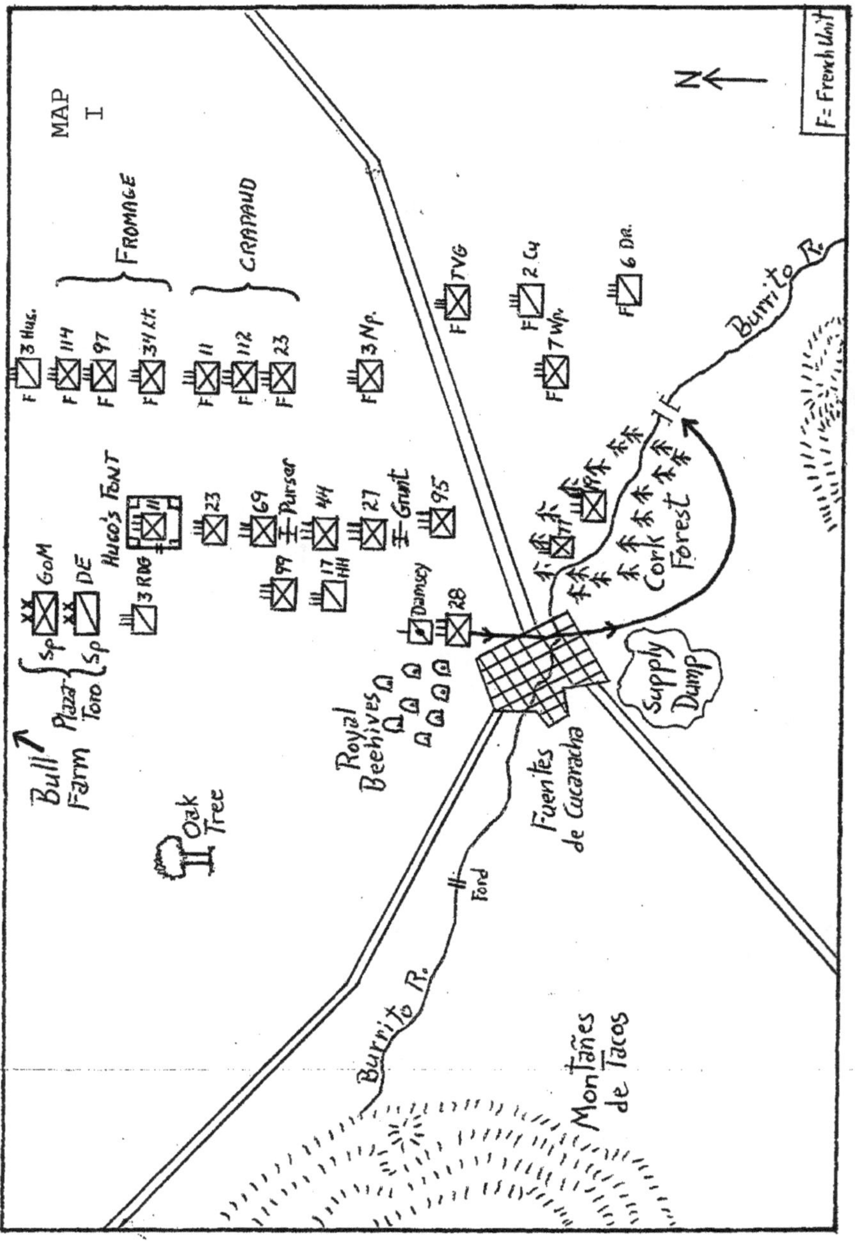

MAP I

F = French Unit

N

FROMAGE
CRAPAUD

F 3 Hus.
F 114
F 97
F 34 Lt.
F 11
F 112
F 23
F 3 Np.
F TVG
F 2 Cu
F 7 Wp.
F 6 Dr.

Bull Farm
Plaza { Sp GoM
Toro { Sp DE
Hugo's Font

3 RDG
23
69
Purser
44
27
Grunt
95
99
17 HH
Dancy
28

Oak Tree

Royal Beehives

Fuentes de Cucaracha

Ford

Burrito R.

Cork Forest

Supply Dump

Montañes de Tacos

Burrito R.

84

As 3,000 Frenchmen marched against them, the Spaniards, led by their commander ("His place was in the fore, O!") immediately spiked their guns, threw down their muskets, and, gibbering in terror, stampeded westward with astonishing speed. Soon only a dwindling cloud of dust indicated that they had ever been present at all.

Sir Marmaduke Doiley met this precipitous departure of two-thirds of his force with the stiff upper lip expected of an English gentleman. Only a few close observers could detect in his demeanor any sign of unease, such as his hair turning white. "How vewwy annoying. I'll wally the beggars," he croaked, and galloped off north. (He did not catch the Spaniards, but he did find a large tree to hide in.)[2]

4. THE DEFENSE OF HUGOSFONT

The Spanish flight (or "tactical withdrawal," as the Duque called it in his AAR) caused the farmhouse and walled garden of Hugosfont to become the left flank of the British line.

Inside the place was the 11th Regiment, the famous Ballyshannon Leprechauns, under Col. O'Malarkey. This unit was recruited from the dregs of County Antrim and officered by outcast Orangemen. Many British regiments boast special distinctions of dress and insignia. That of the 11th was the ball and chain fastened at night around each man's leg to prevent him from deserting.[3] The Leprechauns had been put inside Hugosfont mainly because the farm complex had only one gate, making it easy for nearby troops to guard against mass flight.

As the French 34th *Légère* closed on the farm, a Homeric struggle took place: the frantic efforts of the 11th to get the hell out of there before the French arrived while other British troops tried to hold them in. Action centered at the gate, where two companies of the 23rd Royal Welch Halberdiers (Leekeaters) was stationed to keep it shut.

As French musket balls began splattering the farm's eastern wall, two companies of the 11th rushed the gate. (Serious fighting was avoided since the Leprechauns were armed only with shillelaghs, the English having discovered that half the men were too backward to be taught to fire a musket and the other half used them for self-inflicted wounds.) Baulked here, other Gaels began climbing over the wall while Col. O'Malarkey led his grenadier company in pelting the 23rd with whiskey bottles, of which they had an almost limitless supply. But a few volleys fired into the air and vigorous employment of rifle butts scared the Irishmen back inside, and as the French arrived the 23rd's companies withdrew and left them to their fate.

Col. de Trop, commanding the 34th, approached Hugosfont cautiously: in the absence of enemy fire, he feared some clever trap. In fact the Ballyshannon Leprechauns were cowering in all corners of the building and garden. When the French got within fifty yards, de Trop raised his shako on the point of his sword and yelled, *"En avant, mes braves!"* His men responded with a cry of *"Vive la plume de ma tante!"* and stormed forward.

But the men had no ladders with which to climb the twelve-foot wall. Those who tried to go through one of the four windows were hit on the head (*tête*) by a knobby club. After his men had suffered over twenty concussions, de Trop discovered the gate, but all attempts to open it failed. Col. O'Malarkey, seeing the French could do him little harm, again got his grenadiers throwing bottles over the wall while others dropped their balls and chains onto the discomfited foe.

De Trop sent in his secret weapon, a lieutenant named Hercule Bêtise, reputedly the strongest, and certainly the dumbest, man in the army. Bêtise (called *l'enfonceur*) charged the gate full tilt and rammed his head through it. His comrades widened the breach; a furious scrum ensued between the enraged Gauls and desperate Gaels. A hail of whiskey bottles stunned enough French to allow the gate to be shut and barred. Stymied, Col. de Trop opened fire at the walls and windows while trying to think of some other way to take the obstinate farm.

5. THE FRENCH ENVELOPMENT (0900 - 1200)

While Hugosfont was stormed, the rest of the French attack went smoothly, owing to the rout of Plaza-Toro's men. North of the farm the two other regiments of Fromage's division (97th and 114th) and the 3rd Hussars moved past the strongpoint and began wheeling south. The only British unit in their way was the 3rd (Prince of Wales's Very Own Personal) Royal Dragoon Guards. Its commander, Col. Caltrop, slowly withdrew, hoping someone would send him some orders.

South of Hugosfont, Gen. Crapaud's three regiments, supported by a line of skirmishers and eight guns, began to advance upon the two British regiments to their front. The northernmost of these, the 23rd Royal Welsh Halberdiers (Leekeaters) was a decent unit under the experienced Col. Davies; the regimental silver band was famed throughout the peninsula, while the soldiers' hearty renditions of *Men of Harlech, Calon Lan, Cwm*

Rhondda, and other favorites, had often brought both friends and foes to the verge of distraction.

Unfortunately the 23rd's neighbor unit was less stalwart. Recruited from the cretinous peasantry of southern England, led by wealthy young graduates of famous public schools, the 69th (Essex, Wessex, Sussex, Middlesex, and Homosex) Regiment—usually called the "Queens' Own"—was in Spain only because the notorious behavior of its officers made it expedient to get it out of England.

The center company of the 69th was under Lt. the Hon. Dorian Gay, recently thrown out of Eton for the usual reasons. This decorative young person looked at the approaching French, fluttered his long lashes, and fainted. His swoon precipitated a panic throughout the 69th that spread to the 23rd when a cannonball took off a major's head. Within seconds both regiments were in flight, an unforgettable scene described by the famous Peninsular historian Sir William Rapier:

Then was seen with what strength and majesty the British soldier flees .... Nothing could stop that astonishing infantry. Gen. Doiley, from his tree, shouted frantically, but this only augmented the irremediable disorder, and the mighty mass went headlong up the steep until 987 unwounded men, the remnant of 1,000 British soldiers, stood triumphantly safe upon the distant hills [i.e., the Montañes de Tacos].

Seeing this gap opening in the enemy line, Crapaud's troops rushed forward, cheering and yelling—but the British were not dead yet. As the French regiments became disordered by their advance they were charged by the 17th Heavy Hussars, whose colonel, Fetlock, threw in his men on his own initiative. The gallant cavalry scattered the skirmishers and forced the French to form square. Simultaneously, the 99th (Fife and Drum Yeomanry) marched into the gap and formed line, while the 44th stood firm, supported by Purser's guns.

By noon, then, the French had turned the British left, bent back their line, and were in a position to continue their advance to the river if they overcame a bit more resistance. Hugosfont continued to hold out.

6. THE CENTER AND THE SOUTH (1100-1400)

While all this excitement went on to the north, Gen. L'Heureux came galloping down the road in a vinous stupor, trying to comprehend what was happening around him. Seeing a body of troops he thought to be part of Crapaud's division, he motioned them forward and continued to ride towards the enemy.

The troops he was now leading were in fact an independent unit, the 3rd Neapolitan Infantry (Pasta Fusiliers), a regiment of limited value (to put it mildly). An Italian ruler once said that one could dress his soldiers in red, or blue, or green, but they would run away all the same. He knew his people well. But as the Pasta Fusiliers slowly advanced, they were greatly impressed and heartened by the sight of their general so boldly leading them forward, waving his sword with one hand and his wine bottle with the other, his reins in his teeth. All eyes were on L'Heureux. So when Grunt's howitzer opened fire with shell, and the general disappeared in a pillar of smoke and flame, the Pasta Fusiliers halted in dismay; and when, seconds later, their general emerged to view—horseless, hatless, coatless, shoeless, pantless, his hair on fire—the horrified infantry cried "Mamma mia!" and skedaddled. They were not seen again. Ever.

L'Heureux dazedly walked back to his lines. As an aide extinguished his smoldering *cheveux* the general muttered, "Mille tonneres! Zat wine 'as zome kick, n'est-ce-pas? and called for another horse, another bottle, and another pair of pants.

The southernmost infantry unit in the French front line was the 7th Westphalian Regiment, a group of homesick Germans under Col. von Kaputt. In accordance with orders, the maudlin Jerries began to advance on the cork forest while the 6th Dragoons trotted alongside.

Lurking within the forest was Col. Cower's Royal Yellowjackets ("waspish soldiery"), who began picking off Germans as fast as the men could hammer balls down their Bakers. But the Westphalians, to everyone's surprise, went into open order and continued to advance. As they closed to the woods and the Brits saw the glint of cold steel, Col. Cower, deciding not to sacrifice the chief advantage of his rifles (range), ordered his men to fix swords and discreetly retire to the depths of the leafy glade. With a cry of *ach du lieber Augustin*! the Germans entered the woods.

But all at once the seemingly-victorious 7th was taken under accurate enfilade fire from the trees to its right rear. For attached to the departed 19th was a company of the famous 77th Sussex, Sherwood, and Shropshire Sharpshooters, under Capt. Vyvyan Phipps-Whilloughby. This officer had not received Cower's retreat order, and his highly-trained marksmen peppered von Kaputt's men, who could not see their assailants.[4] Westphalian morale sank and the Germans hastily withdrew in confusion from the suddenly-inhospitable forest.

As the Germans reached the plain they were startled to see a British regiment, accompanied by artillery, crossing the nearby bridge. This was Trimble's 28th (Gardenshires) with Capt. Norman Damsey's RHA battery in support.

This alarming development was also seen by Col. Fauxpas and his 6th Dragoons. Not losing a second, he ordered a charge, which was joined by the 2nd Cuirassiers (Col. Parbleu).

Trimble formed square while the guns struggled to get into firing position. The Gardenshires were a green unit; but despite some men firing away their ramrods, the regiment resisted gallantly. Damsey's battery was engulfed by dragoons, but a few moments later Trimble's men witnessed a heartening sight. Again Sir William Rapier

Suddenly the multitude [of French cavalry] became violently agitated, an English shout pealed high and clear, the mass was rent asunder, and Norman Damsey burst forth sword in hand at the head of his battery. His horses breathing fire, stretched like greyhounds along the plain, the guns bounded behind him like things of no weight, and the mounted gunners followed close, heads bent low and pointed weapons in desperate career.[5]

Damsey halted just east of the bridge. Unfortunately his horses had breathed so much fire that they all dropped dead, while the reason his guns had bounded like weightless things is that four of his six cannon had fallen off their carriages during his wild retreat. But the two remaining were manhandled into firing position, and their fire, with the brave resistance of the 28th and the accurate sniping of the 77th SS&SS from the edge of the woods, forced the discomfited French cavalry to withdraw and held back von Kaputt's 7th Regiment.

7. CHARGE AND COUNTERCHARGE (1200-1400)

At noon the British situation was on the whole desperate. Though the right was holding, the left and center were in grave danger. The divisions of Crapaud and Fromage were advancing steadily, pushing back and outflanking the thin red line. [See Map II]

The 99th and 44th Regiments slid left to confront Fromage; the 27th, (Haggis Highlanders, Colonel McMacCameronargyllgordon), facing nothing since the flight of the Neapolitans, moved north to face Crapaud. Purser's battery swung round to blast Crapaud. But this would not be enough. Clearly the British—as so often in history—needed some deus ex machina (akin to the arrival of Blücher at Waterloo or the German pause before Dunkirk). The Archbishop of Canterbury's Own was praying for a miracle.

*

When, shortly after dispatching Doiley, the future Duke of Wellington learned that the talented Lt. Col. Potts, Doiley's chief of staff, had fallen ill, he realized that Doiley would probably get into trouble. He therefore decided to send to his aid a really good cavalry unit, the 1st Life Guards. Setting out a day after Doiley left, the Life Guards (as luck would have it) now arrived on the field, unexpected by either side. Their leader, Lord Belgrave-Square, saw that he was perfectly positioned to attack the enemy right rear, and instantly drew up his 500 sabers (as well as his men and horses) for a powerful charge.

The Life Guards made a gallant show as they thundered forward, crimson swimming trunks and gold-lamé bathing caps glistening in the sun, flippered feet urging on their spirited mounts, the colonel's distinctive silver snorkel raised on high. Forward they rushed in wild career, their horses breathing fire (as was the wont of horses in those bold times) and crash they went into the 3rd Hussars and Fromage's left flank.

The customary horrid carnage ensued.

Seeing the French in trouble, other British units attacked: the 3rd Royal Dragoon Guards, the 99th Fife and Drums, and the 17th Heavy Hussars. (Some men of the 99th, in their eagerness to enter the fray, grabbed the cavalrymen's stirrups. The cavalry not so impeded, however, continued to charge.) From a large oak tree on the fringe of the melee a lisping voice called encouragement to the British; in fact, things now seemed to be going so well that several soldiers saw the pasty physiognomy of their commander emerge amidst the leaves.

All at once an even more dramatic development developed. The bulls in the corral north of the battlefield had been growing more and more restless throughout the noisy day and were further excited by the motion of all the red uniforms. An especially gigantic bull, *el toro furiente*, now launched a charge of his own, followed by dozens of his colleagues.

This taurine onslaught fell with dread effect on both sides. Fromage's division, half the British infantry, the Life Guards and other cavalry, were all thrown into utter confusion and swept away towards the Burrito. The crazed horses swam the river and vanished, while the soldiers were left scattered and utterly disorganized over a wide area.

8. VICTORY FROM DEFEAT, AND VICE-VERSA (1400-1500)

With the disappearance of the western flank of each army, the failure of the French attack on the British right, and the slowing of Crapaud's attack by the gallant resistance of the 44th and the Haggis Highlanders, the crisis of the battle had arrived. The center of what was left of the British line was held only by Col. Wall-Nutt's thinly-spread 95th Regiment (Worcestershire and Horseradish), supported by Grunt's battery. If the French could break through here, they could yet prevail.

This was clear even to Gen. L'Heureux, who, now remounted (and re-clothed), sat sipping brandy near the road. He knew this was the time to commit his ultimate reserve. He gave the order, "*La Garde au feu!*"

This command sent forward the 1st Regiment of Imperial Guard Grenadier Pensioners. Popularly known as the *Trés Vielle Garde*, or the "Oldest of the Oldest," it consisted of 700 men combed out of the Invalides and other military retirement hospitals after 1812, when the Emperor needed every man he could get.[6]

Wearing impressive tall fur nightcaps, armed with weighted canes, these aged but still-gallant relics now tottered forward. As they boldly advanced with hoarse shouts of *Vive... j'oublie quoi*, all eyes were on them. (These eyes included those of Sir Marmaduke Doiley, whose staff, fearful of losing their cushy jobs if their boss was cashiered for timidity, had coaxed him down from his tree by threats that, unless he descended, they would not give him his nightly caning, a threat no public-school man would lightly disregard.)

Grunt's battery opened fire on the T.V.G., employing not only round shot but Congreve rockets—those ingenious but erratic contrivances that occasionally produced unexpected results. Certainly here at Fuentes de Cucaracha the Congreve rocket could be said to have had a decisive effect. One of them sailed up in a great arc, reversed course, and descended with a fiery explosion amidst the Royal Beehives.

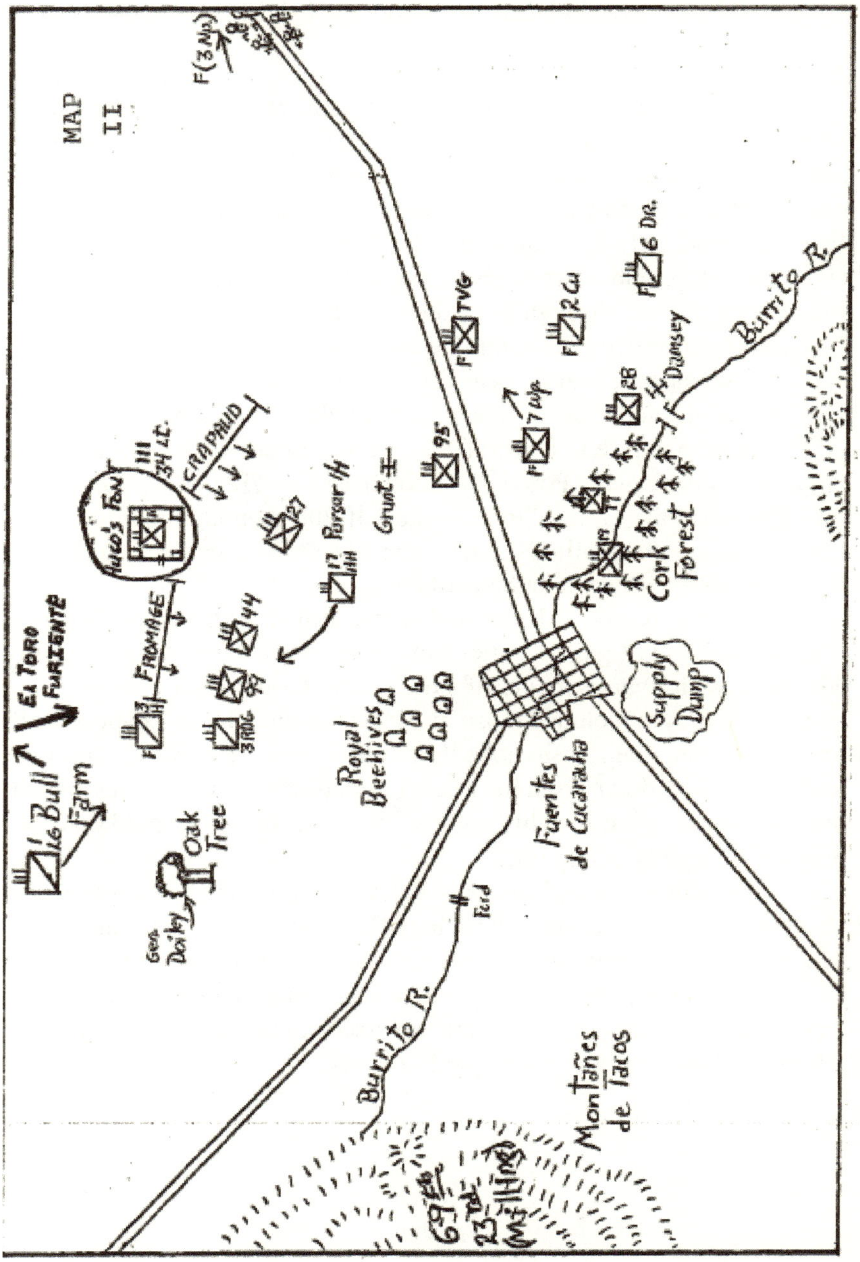

MAP II

F (3 Mts)

16 Bull Farm

1 16 Bull

El Toro Furiente

Gen. Dolley

Oak Tree

Auto's Font

III 34 Lt.

CRAPAUD

F 3 Hj FROMAGE

27

17 Porpar H

17 Hh

44

3 Roc.

Royal Beehives

Grunt

95

TVG

F

F 7 up

7 up

2 w

F 2 w

28

Supply Dump

4 Dumsey

6 Dr.

F 6 Dr.

Cork Forest

Burite R.

Fuentes de Cucaracha

Ford

Burite R.

Montañes de Tacos

69

23 Tel.
(Milling)

92

In moments, the ears of all combatants were smitten by a furious humming as clouds of irate bees enveloped the battlefield. The bayonets and muskets of mankind were of no avail against apian stilettos. Gallic cries of *sauve qui peut*! were echoed by another English shout pealing high and clear: run for your lives! Amidst screams of "ouch" and "eek" the armies dissolved into fleeing mobs. The enraged bees also swarmed over Hugosfont, where the reluctantly-gallant Ballyshannon Leprechauns, having run out of whiskey bottles, were about to surrender. The 34th Light ran away and the Irishmen took refuge in rooms and cellars

*.

So ended the Battle of Fuentes de Cucaracha, and a mighty struggle it had been. Although casualties were not high after the various routed units reassembled—about 500 French and 350 British—both armies were crippled by stings and had to withdraw to their main bodies.

The French supplies—remember the supplies?—were devoured or sold by the local populace.

*

General Doiley decided to send in his papers and return to England, where his wealth and noble friends assured him a long career in Parliament; he was a figure of some note, or notoriety, during the reign of George IV; he died suddenly in 1832, aged 58, of a heart attack caused by passage of the Reform Bill (which eliminated his borough).

General L'Heureux was retired from the army in 1814 (for some reason). When Napoleon returned from Elba, L'Heureux rallied to him but received a note saying that the best way he could help the Emperor would be to offer his services to Louis XVIII. L'Heureux never recovered from this blow; he returned to obscurity in Perpignan, emerging every so often to win a drinking contest. He passed away in 1834, aged 67, apparently from spontaneous combustion.

----

[1] Ivry is, as every schoolboy knows, the site of Henry IV's great victory over the Catholic League in 1590.

[2] "Doiley's Oak" still stands near the town.

[3] The ball was stamped with a shamrock and the motto "Quis separabit?" Officers had golden chains, NCOs silver, other ranks brass.

[4] It is well known that the 95th Rifles wore dark green uniforms to give concealment in woods. The 77th SS&SS improved on this, the men being dressed as giant squirrels.

[5] It is unnecessary to parody Gen. Napier; one merely quotes him.

[6] In contrast to the "Marie Louises," or young draftees, the *Trés Vielle Garde* was sometimes called the "Madame Pompadours". The regiment is an interesting contrast to another unit organized at the same time in the ever-burgeoning Guard, the *Trés Jeune Garde*, which was unique among French regiments in having nannies instead of vivandiéres.

ABOUT THE AUTHOR

I was born in Maine in 1949, studied at Johns Hopkins (B.A.), UMass (M.A.), and Purdue (Ph.D.; fields: European military and diplomatic history and modern Germany), and have taught at a prep school in Minnesota (Shattuck-St. Mary's) since 1978.

I went part-time in 2000, mainly so I could write. First I published *And Gladly Teach*, a satirical novel about a fictional prep school. Then I started a fantasy-adventure series, *Mercenaries*.

I hoped for traditional publication of *Storm Approaching*, the first volume in the series, and was lucky enough to get a fine agent; but even fine agents are not always successful, as you can read in Essay 24.

Storm Approaching was succeeded by *Gold and Glory, Resolution,* and *The Free Lands*.

"Merchandising" self-published books is difficult. I hope readers of this volume will be tempted to try my novels. (If you like them, buy several and give them to your friends. If you dislike them, buy even more and give them to your enemies.)

Why do I write? I could quote J.R.R.T. ("The prime motive was the desire of a tale-teller to try his hand at a really long story that would hold the attention of readers, amuse them, delight them, and at times maybe excite or deeply move them") or I could quote Samuel Johnson ("No man but a blockhead ever wrote, except for money"). I think I agree with both these masters.

Please favor my blog with a visit: andiriel.blogspot.com

www.ingramcontent.com/pod-product-compliance
Lightning Source LLC
Chambersburg PA
CBHW020950030426
42339CB00004B/30